*RESTORATION
CARNIVAL*

DORSET

ROCHESTER

SEDLEY

SHEFFIELD

ETHEREGE

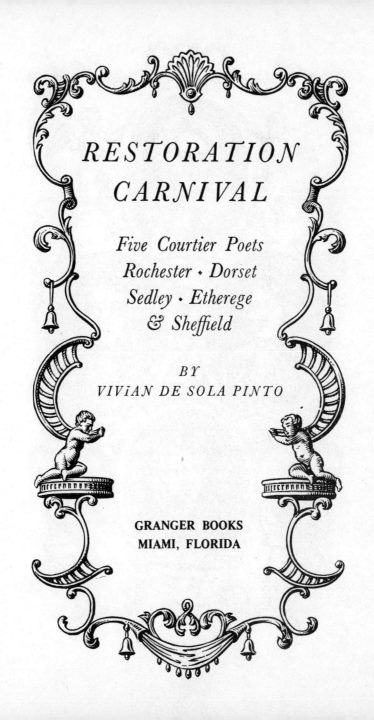

RESTORATION CARNIVAL

Five Courtier Poets
Rochester · Dorset
Sedley · Etherege
& Sheffield

BY
VIVIAN DE SOLA PINTO

GRANGER BOOKS
MIAMI, FLORIDA

First Published 1954
Reprinted 1976

Frontispiece and title-page border by T. L. Poulton
Ornaments and initials from Plantin's 'Index Characterum'

PRINTED IN THE UNITED STATES OF AMERICA

Contents

when Night
Darkens the Streets, then wander forth the Sons
Of Belial, *flown with insolence and wine.*

MILTON, Paradise Lost, I, 500–502

Then our Age was in it's Prime,
Free from Rage, and free from Crime,
A very Merry, Dancing, Drinking,
Laughing, Quaffing, and unthinking Time.

JOHN DRYDEN, The Secular Masque, 1700

Lord, what would they say
Should their Catullus walk that way?

W. B. YEATS, The Scholars

Preface

When Pope in his 'Epistle to Augustus' wrote of

> the Wits of either Charles's days,
> The Mob of Gentlemen who wrote with Ease;
> Sprat, Carew, Sedley, and a hundred more,
> (Like twinkling stars the Miscellanies o'er)...

he was looking back to the last age in England when poetry still formed an essential part of the life of a courtier and when a court still produced verses as a matter of course. It is true that he does not distinguish between the wits of the reigns of Charles I and of Charles II. In our own time Dr F. R. Leavis has made some very acute observations on the differences between the wits of the period before the 'troubles' with their 'old rich court culture' and the wits of the Restoration Court.[1] No doubt he is right in his contention that much of that fine court culture failed to survive the interregnum and that in a very real sense the poetry of the Restoration Court represents, to use his own expression, 'the decay of the Caroline courtly tradition'. Still the poetry of the Restoration wits is the last body of English verse which was produced by a court, which, with all its shortcomings, still regarded itself not merely as a fashionable club but as an ideal community embodying certain qualities of grace and fine living and which was also in touch with a genuine popular culture of the street and the tavern. A last faint pathetic echo of that alliance can be heard in the 'pale and vapid songs, long out of date, about Chloe, and Phyllis, and Strephon' sung by Old Mr Nandy in Dickens's 'Little Dorrit'

[1] 'Revaluation' (1936), p. 34.

The poetry of the Restoration wits has not hitherto been easily accessible, and it therefore seems desirable that a representative selection of it should be presented to the public as the work of a group in a setting of the lives of some of the chief courtier-poets. The work of scholars in England and America has done much in recent years to clear up the thick veil of gossip, scandal and synthetic romance which has shrouded the lives and reputations of these men for two centuries. It is time that use was made of this work to present them to the public, not, indeed, as major writers, but as a group with considerable historical significance, and the authors of a body of verse of permanent value, worthy to be studied beside the best comedies of the period and the 'Diary' of Samuel Pepys as an expression of an extremely interesting phase of English culture.

The texts of the poems presented in this collection reproduce the spelling, capitalisation and punctuation of the original editions, except for the correction of obvious misprints and the substitution of the modern 's' for the old long 'ſ'. In the few poems printed from contemporary MSS the abbreviations have been expanded as they would have been in contemporary editions. I wish to thank the Duke of Portland and the University of Nottingham for permission to print two manuscript poems by Rochester in the Portland Collection now in Nottingham University Library and Mr Charles Ede of the Folio Society for his kind and valuable help in the preparation of this book for the press.

V. DE SOLA PINTO

UNIVERSITY OF NOTTINGHAM, 1954

Introduction

THE RESTORATION of the monarchy in 1660 meant, among other things, the revival of the English court. In spite of the upheaval of the Civil War, the great courtly tradition of the Renaissance remained alive at Whitehall, the ancient palace which the Stuart kings had inherited from their Tudor predecessors. The court of Charles II was the last English court to be a real centre of culture as well as of fashion. At the Tudor courts, in the words of Professor Trevelyan, 'the gentlemen of England learned not only the intrigues of love and politics, but music and poetry, and a taste for scholarship and the arts'. The ideal of the Renaissance courtier described by Baldassare Castiglione in his book *Il Cortegiano* was realised in Elizabeth's reign by such men as Sir Philip Sidney, and was immortalised by Shakespeare in the character of Hamlet with his 'courtier's, soldier's, scholar's eye, tongue, sword'. It was a great ideal and its realisation was, perhaps, possible only at a great moment in history, the High Renaissance of Shakespeare, Michelangelo and Cervantes. Already in the Elizabethan age Spenser had noted the appearance of a new type of courtier whose aim in life was not devotion to high ideals of loyalty, service and humane culture but the gratification of every sensuous appetite. In his *Mother Hubberds Tale*, after describing the 'rightful courtier', the poet contrasts him with the young gallants led astray by the Ape, who is the symbol of vice:

> But the yong lustie gallants he did chose
> To follow, meete to whom he might disclose

His witlesse pleasance, and ill pleasing vaine.
A thousand wayes he them could entertaine,
With all the thriftles games that may be found
With mumming and with masking all around,
With dice, with cards, with balliards, farre unfit,
With shuttlecocks, misseeming manlie wit,
With courtizans, and costlie riotize. . . .[1]

Such complaints about the degeneration of court life had, indeed, been made long before Spenser. The court had always
contained in itself two possibilities. It could be the nursery of
culture, of learning and of statesmanship, and it could be a
very pleasant club of idle pleasure-seekers, *le monde où on
s'amuse*. There is no doubt whatever that since the death of
Elizabeth it tended more and more towards the second of
these two alternatives. An anonymous popular poet of the
reign of James I makes an ironic comparison between an old
courtier of the queen and the king's new courtier. Here is the
courtier of the new age:

With a new flourishing gallant, new come to his land,
Who kept a brace of new painted creatures to his command,
And could take up a thousand readily upon his new bond
And be drunk at a new Tavern till he be not able to go or stand,
    Like a new Courtier of the King's
    And the King's new Courtier.
    .   .   .   .

With a new study stuffed full of pamphlets and plays
And a new pedagogue Chaplain that swears faster than he
        prays
And a new buttery hatch that opens once in five or six days,
And a new French Cook to devise kickshaws and toys,
    Like a new Courtier of the King's
    And the King's new Courtier.

[1] Spenser, *Mother Hubberds Tale*, ll. 797–805.

This description, though written before the Civil War, might have been a prophecy of the new courtiers of 1660, seen through by the jaundiced eyes of a survivor from the Elizabethan court. When Charles II came back to Whitehall he chose as his favourite companions neither the old servants of his father nor the Presbyterian leaders who combined with them to restore the monarchy. The chosen friends of the new king were George Villiers, duke of Buckingham, Dryden's Zimri, that volatile nobleman who

> In the course of one revolving Moon,
> Was Chymist, Fidler, States-man, and Buffoon.

and a group of younger men who were nicknamed the 'merry gang'. They were, in the words of Burnet, 'the three most eminent wits of that time, on whom all the lively libels were fastened . . . the earls of Dorset and Rochester and Sir Charles Sidley'. As a matter of fact, Rochester was a boy of thirteen at the time of the Restoration. It was only after his return from his travels on the Continent in December 1664 that he became a prominent member of the nightly congregation at court. Closely associated with these four men were Harry Killigrew, Harry Savile, Dick Newport and Fleetwood, and Shepherd. A brilliant addition to the society was a pale-faced, debauched-looking young man called George Etherege (nicknamed Gentle George), who became acquainted with Lord Buckhurst (afterwards earl of Dorset) through the success of his play *The Comical Revenge*. These young men shocked the old-fashioned Cavaliers like the Duke of Ormonde and the Earl of Clarendon by their boldness of speech and irreverence. In 1661 Ormonde told Clarendon that 'the king spent most of his time with confident young men who abhorred all discourse that was serious, and, in the liberty they assumed in drollery and raillery, preserved no reverence towards God or man, but laughed at all sober men, and even at religion itself'.[1] Clarendon wrote that among these young men of the post-war generation 'the tenderness of the bowels, which is the quintessence of justice and compassion, the very mention of good nature was laughed at and looked upon as the mark or character of a fool; and a roughness of manners, or hardheadedness and cruelty was affected'.[2]

These are the hostile opinions of old-fashioned observers, but there is much to be said on the other side. The young courtiers of the Restoration were brought up in a very different England from the England of Sidney and Spenser, different even from the England of Charles I and the young Edward Hyde. It was a nation which had been rent in two by the Civil War, a confused struggle, partly political and partly religious. The great majority of both parties in that struggle were unsympathetic to liberal and humane ideals. Although there were Miltons and Marvells who served the protector, and Jeremy Taylors and Henry Vaughans who served the king, the majority of Cavaliers and the majority of Roundheads were unlovely enough—'Publicans on one side and Pharisees on the other'. What could be more natural than that high-spirited, intelligent, wealthy young men belonging to a privileged class, with a good education, as education went in those days, should say 'a plague o' both your houses', and try the experiment of building up a little pagan paradise of pleasure? It was an age of experiment, and both Rochester and Sedley had received part of their education at Wadham College, Oxford, the cradle of the Royal Society and the new scientific movement. They all read and admired the works of Thomas Hobbes, the materialist philosopher who had been tutor to Charles II. If Hobbes was right and the universe consisted of atoms governed by mechanical laws, surely it was only sensible to enjoy the good things of this world and ignore

[1] Clarendon, *Life*, vol. I, pp. 354, 355.
[2] *Ibid.* p. 307.

the croakings of the kill-joys, whether they were Puritan preachers, old Cavalier noblemen or Anglican parsons.

The court at Whitehall Palace was full of gaiety and colour. Charles II, the tall, swarthy, witty, amorous king, with an immense appetite for pleasure and a hatred for stiffness and formality, was the incarnate spirit of the place. His trumpeters and kettle-drummers marched through the park in scarlet and gold, his courtiers and mistresses rustled through the galleries in the silks and satins which we can still see in Lely's portraits. Paintings by the great Italian and Flemish masters hung on the walls of the palace, and in its chambers flutes, oboes and violins were for ever discoursing the music of Henry Lawes, of Purcell, of Lully and of Grabut. Not far away on the north side of the Strand were Covent Garden and Drury Lane, the new bohemia of theatres, taverns and coffeehouses. Here were 'idle places and lanes' full of 'abundance of loose women' standing at the doors. Here were the 'brisk blades' or 'town gallants', with their great white periwigs, lolling on the benches of the new modish play-houses and listening to Mr Betterton and the pretty, pert actresses speaking the verses of Shakespeare or of Mr Dryden and the choice prose of Gentle George Etherege. Farther east was Whetstone Park, where Mother Creswell, the procuress, and her like, sold strong waters and fresh-faced wenches to all who had guineas to buy them. This world of beauty and music, of colour and squalor and vice, was the background of the lives of the 'merry gang' or the 'flashy fry', as Rochester calls them, and here in the 1660's and the 1670's they built their pagan paradise—'A very Merry, Dancing, Drinking, Laughing, Quaffing, and unthinking Time', as Dryden called it in his *Secular Masque* (1700). But it is unfair to the 'merry gang' to represent them as mere fribbles and pleasure-seekers. They were men of real culture, artists in living and artists in words. They read and loved the Latin poets and

often translated them admirably. They knew contemporary
French literature well, and they delighted in Shakespeare
and the old English drama. Music and the theatre were among
their principal pleasures, and they enjoyed critical discus-
sions with men of letters like Dryden, Shadwell and Wycherley. It is significant that, when Dryden wrote his great critical
dialogue *Of Dramatick Poesie*, he chose two of the 'merry
gang' as his principal interlocutors, and the arguments he
puts into their mouths probably represent their conversation
accurately enough. They were not only literary courtiers,
they were also Bohemian men of letters in touch with the
life of the street, the tavern and the coffee-house, the rough
democracy of seventeenth-century London.

The Restoration carnival of the society of wits lasted until
about the end of the second decade after the king's return. In
the 1670's the health of Rochester, who had the most powerful
and acute mind and the frailest body of all the members of
the group, was breaking down. Like Dryden's Achitophel,
he was

> A fiery Soul, which, working out its way,
> Fretted the Pigmy Body to decay:
> And o'r-informed the Tenement of Clay.

At the same time, his mature intelligence perceived that the
little pagan paradise was an impossible ideal. He saw that *le
monde où on s'amuse* was surrounded on all sides by the
rottenness, ugliness and corruption revealed by his friend
William Wycherley in his powerful satiric comedies. So he
used his brilliant gifts to satirise the stupidity, greed and
cruelty of his contemporaries, and finally in his greatest poem
attacked mankind and reason itself. Seeking a more positive
and satisfying philosophy than the materialism of Hobbes, he
turned first to deism, the 'religion of Nature', and finally to
Christianity, whole-heartedly rejecting in the last months of
his life the epicurean experiment of his youth, and dying a

sincere convert to the religion which he had formerly mocked and flouted. Sedley, who had a less powerful and original mind, was a man of sense and intelligence in spite of his youthful pranks; and after a severe illness he reconstructed his life, became an active and useful member of Parliament, and an excellent father, transforming himself successfully from a Restoration wit to an Augustan gentleman. Gentle George became a diplomat, but remained a typical Restoration wit till the end. His letters from Ratisbon, where he represented James II till 1688, are full of laments for the changes that had come over his old friends and of nostalgic longings for the days of Charles II: 'Few of us', he writes, 'have the gift to be constant to ourselves. Sir Ch: Sidlie setts up for good houres, and sobriety: my Ld Dorset has given over variety, and shuts himself up within my Lady's arms.'[1]

When the Revolution of 1688 put an end to a phase of English history and the long period of the domination of the middle class and money power began, the golden age of the 'merry gang' was already a legend, but it was an inspiration to a young man of genius called William Congreve, who came to London from Ireland in 1690, and soon won the friendship of the great John Dryden. The basis of his great comedies was the tradition of the aristocratic paradise of wit and pleasure of the courtier-poets of the reign of Charles II. *Love for Love* and *The Way of the World* are irradiated by the sunset glow of the last English court which was the centre of a vital and creative culture. After that the wits were remembered for generations as bogy-men of wickedness who defied all the laws of middle-class respectability. Now we can judge their lives dispassionately in relation to the standards of the age in which they lived and through the music of their verses we can participate in their joyous vision of a 'Utopia

[1] Letter to Henry Guy, Ratisbon, 19 December 1687 (*The Letter Book of Sir George Etherege*, B.M. Add. MS. 11513, f. 153 v).

of gallantry, where pleasure is duty, and the manners perfect freedom'.[1]

Lyric poetry was an essential part of the life of seventeenth-century England. It was to be found everywhere, in the streets where the itinerant ballad-singers, male and female, sang and vended their wares, in the taverns where broadside verses were stuck on the walls and catches were roared by the topers, at the theatre where no play was complete without several songs, at the booksellers', where innumerable anthologies of popular lyrics like the Drolleries and the Academies of Compliments sold like hot cakes, in private houses where, in Milton's words, 'airs and madrigalls' whispered 'softnes in chambers',[2] and, above all, at court, where the composition of songs was a necessary accomplishment of every gentleman, and the singing of them, or the listening to them, was the common recreation of both sexes. In fact, to judge from contemporary plays, the singing of a song by a servant, a music master or a friend with a good voice was used very much as the wireless set is used today. When the conversation flagged, the music was turned on, and the music was that of lyric verse and the human voice. In Congreve's *The Old Bachelor* the music master Gavot enters and is at once asked to sing 'the last new song'. 'O, I am glad we shall have a song to divert the discourse!', Araminta exclaims. In Etherege's *The Comical Revenge* the melancholy Graciana asks the waiting maid Letitia to sing to her, and

With thy sweet voice refresh my wearied soul.

When Sir Fopling Flutter, in Etherege's *The Man of Mode*, makes his debut in London society on his return from Paris,

---

[1] Charles Lamb, 'On the Artificial Comedy of the Last Century', in *Essays of Elia*.
[2] *Areopagitica* (1644).

one of his first preoccupations is the composition of a song, his 'Coup d'Essay in English'.

In the reign of Charles II, according to the Earl of Rochester the 'three buisinisses of the age' were 'Woemen, Polliticks and Drinking'.[1] The first and last of these were the chief subjects of the lyrical poems of the wits. The lyric was part of the traditional technique of courtship. It was a tradition that went back to the troubadours and the *amour courtois* of the Middle Ages. Fashions in the love lyric changed like fashions in dress. From the time of Wyatt to that of Shakespeare the sugared sonnets of Petrarch were the vogue. They were succeeded by the 'metaphysical' wit of the school of Donne. Already before the Civil War Ben Jonson had set the fashion for clarity, neatness, simplicity and classic proportion. The Latin poets Horace, Catullus and Martial were now the favourite models, and their example was reinforced by that of the elegant verses of contemporary French poets, Racan, Malherbe, Voiture, Sarasin and Madame de La Suze. John Sheffield, in his *Essay on Poetry* (1682), sums up the Restoration ideal:

> First then, of *Songs*, that now so much abound,
> Without his Song no Fop is to be found,
> A most offensive Weapon which he draws,
> On all he meets, against *Apollo*'s Laws:
> Though nothing seems more easy, yet no part
> Of Poetry requires a nicer Art;
> For as in rows of richest Pearl there lyes
> Many a blemish that escapes our Eyes,
> The least of which Defects is plainly shewn
> In one small Ring, and brings the value down;
> So Songs should be to just perfection wrought,

---

[1] Letter to H. Savile, 22 June 1674 (*Rochester-Savile Letters*, ed. J. H. Wilson, p. 33).

Yet where can one be seen without a fault;
Exact propriety of words and thought?
Th'expression easy, and the fancy high,
Yet that not seem to creep, nor this to fly;
No words transpos'd, but in such just cadance,
As, though hard wrought, may seem the effect of
  chance.[1]

Sheffield's ideal is a perfect ease of expression that will simulate the natural flow of colloquial speech, combined with a perfection of form like that of a jewel without a flaw. His emphasis is all on style and form, and he says nothing of matter. When Dorimant, in Etherege's play, ironically praises Sir Fopling's 'Coup d'Essay', he says almost the same thing in a few words: 'There is not much thought in't. But 'tis passionate and well turn'd.' The dangers for writers of lyrics who tried to live up to this ideal were aridity and insipidity. An aristocratic clique dominated by a bookish conception of the classic lyric might easily produce work that was 'correct' but lifeless. Both defects are to be found in the poems of Wentworth Dillon, Earl of Roscommon, a writer who is not represented in this collection. This is the nobleman of whom Pope wrote:

In all Charles's days
Roscommon only boasts unspotted lays.

Roscommon was a very respectable person and his lays were perfectly 'unspotted', but they are singularly dull. They are either insipid trifles like his poem *On the Death of a Lady's Dog* or ponderous translations from the Latin. His only readable poems are his version of the *Dies Iræ*, any moderately competent version of which is bound to preserve something of the nobility of the original, and his *Essay on Translated Verse*, which shows some critical ability. The best lyrics were

[1] Buckinghamshire, *An Essay on Poetry* (1682), pp. 5, 6.

certainly written by the 'wicked' courtiers, because they had
a zest for living that the virtuous dilettante lacked and a background of experience in tavern, street, theatre and brothel
which saved them from the aridity of the bookish recluse.
Sedley and Sheffield, indeed, did not wholly avoid the danger
of insipidity, the great snare for writers of love lyrics in the
pastoral tradition. Sometimes their verses are not very far
removed from Etherege's exquisite parody of the fashionable
love lyric in Sir Fopling Flutter's song:

> How Charming *Phillis* is, how fair!
> Ah that she were as willing,
> To ease my wounded heart of Care
> And make her Eyes less killing.

But in their best poems the wits are saved from this kind of
thing by their realistic temper, their humour and their irony.
Their lyrics are all occasional poems, not studied set-pieces.
Their virtues are those which Locker-Lampson described
admirably in the Preface to his *Lyra Elegantiarum* (1867):

'Occasional Verse should seem entirely spontaneous:
when the reader thinks to himself, "I could have written
that, and easily, too", he pays the author a very high compliment, but, at the same time, it is right to observe, that this
absence of effort, as recognised in most works of real excel-
lence, is only apparent; the writing of Occasional Verse is
a difficult accomplishment, for a large number of authors,
both famous and obscure, have attempted it, but in the
majority of cases with very indifferent success, and no one
has fully succeeded who did not possess a certain gift of
irony, which is not only a much rarer quality than humour,
or even wit, but is less commonly met with than is sometimes
imagined.'

It is the combination of this irony with lyric sweetness,
'the sense of musical delight', that distinguishes the best

songs of the wits. Rochester achieves this combination in a number of his lyrics, which have a freshness and crystalline clarity worthy of Catullus or Heine:

> While on those lovely looks I gaze,
> To see a Wretch persuing;
> In Raptures of a blest amaze,
> His pleasing happy Ruine;
> 'Tis not for pity that I move;
> His Fate is too aspiring,
> Whose heart broke with a load of Love,
> Dies wishing and admiring.

The irony of the poem is in the contrast between the passionate intensity of the poet's love and his detached perception of the humour of his own situation—'His pleasing happy Ruine'. Sedley occasionally produces similar effects, using a very simple, unfigured style, as in the Song on p. 70.
$_t$ This is poetry of the kind which Landor called 'diaphanous'. The language is that of conversation, not of 'the middle and lower classes'[1] but of the 'man of sense', the educated gentleman of the day. It is poetry without ornament, naked and limpid as clear water. Such poetry is rare in England, where the fashionable styles have commonly been richly laden with metaphor. When Prosper Mérimée read a French translation of the Russian poet Pushkin to Flaubert, the great stylist said: 'Il est plat, votre poète.' He might have said the same thing if he had read a literal prose translation of the songs of the Restoration wits. But, like Pushkin's poems, when read in the original language, they are not really 'flat' but clear and bright and sparkling.

The love lyric in England, as in other European countries at this time, was dominated by the convention of the rococo

---

[1] Wordsworth, Preface to *Lyrical Ballads*, 1798.

pastoral. The pastoral tradition of Theocritus and Virgil, which had appeared to the eyes of the great men of the Renaissance charged with imaginative splendour, had undergone a curious transformation by the second half of the seventeenth century. The shepherds and shepherdesses had lost their grandeur and had become slim, dainty, elegant figures. When Spenser called Ralegh the 'Shepherd of the Ocean', the word 'shepherd' was filled with high poetic significance. It connoted a man of godlike power living in a world of superhuman grandeur. *Lycidas* was, perhaps, the last English poem in which the pastoral convention had this lofty meaning. For the new generation, writing poetry in the years that followed the Restoration, the pastoral implied an imaginary existence in a non-moral dream-world of delicate grace and charm. The transition is from the shepherds of Virgil and Milton to the *bergeries* of Watteau and Fragonard. The rococo pastoral, as we may call it to distinguish it from the classical or Renaissance pastoral, can easily become silly. It had become silly when Congreve's Lady Wishfort wanted to 'retire to deserts and solitudes and feed harmless sheep by groves and purling streams', and when Pope wrote his delicious parody:

> Mild Arcadians ever blooming,
>   Nightly nodding o'er your Flocks,
> See my weary Days consuming,
>   All beneath yon flow'ry Rocks.

But in the reign of Charles II the rococo pastoral, though it may be sophisticated, is not necessarily silly. It can still be in some degree the symbol of an ideal sort of life, not indeed a ofty, ethical ideal like that of Spenser or Milton, but the truly poetic ideal of a delicate, courtly existence in a gracious world like that of Sidney's Arcadia with its 'Shepheards boy piping as though he would never be old'. Sedley and Sheffield can both use the rococo pastoral admirably because they feel all its charm and do not trouble to think too much about it. Sedley can sometimes produce a picture that Watteau might have painted against a background of great, sombre trees and silvery sky:

> Walking among thick Shades alone,
> I heard a distant Voice,
> Which, sighing, said, Now she is gone,
> I'll make no second Choice.
>
> I look't and saw it was a Swain,
> Who to the flying Wind,
> Did of some neighbouring Nymph complain,
> Too fair, and too unkind.

Rochester, in one remarkable poem (see p. 190), constructed a pastoral group of a nymph and shepherd which suggests the dramatic effects of the contemporary sculpture of Bernini.

The wits, however, lived in an age of realism and mathematics, the age of Descartes, of Hobbes and of Newton. They often deliberately flout the tradition of the faithful, languishing swain and the cruel shepherdess. They are 'men of sense' and, even into their dream-world, they bring a note of actuality. Sedley frankly tells his Phillis to make the best of love while she can, and recognise that it is stuff that will not endure:

> *Phillis*, let's shun the common Fate,
> And let our Love ne'r turn to Hate;
> I'll dote no longer than I can,
> Without being call'd a faithless Man.
> When we begin to want Discourse,
> And kindness seems to tast of Force,
> As freely as we met, we'll part,
> Each one possest of their own Heart.

Rochester asks his Cloris to treat sexual passion in a rational way:

> Such perfect Bliss, fair *Cloris*, we
>   In our Enjoyment prove:
> 'Tis pity restless Jealousie
>   Should mingle with our Love.
>
> Let us, since Wit has taught us how,
>   Raise Pleasure to the Top:
> You Rival Bottle must allow,
>   I'le suffer Rival Fop.

No doubt 'hard-boiled' poems like these shocked the old Cavaliers quite as much as the wildest escapades of the 'merry gang'. Perhaps, however, some of their most delightful effects are produced when they treat the pastoral dream-world with a delicate irony which does not preclude a real appreciation of its charm. Sedley does this several times, notably in his most famous song:

> *Phillis* is my only Joy,
>   Faithless as the Winds or Seas;
> Sometimes coming, sometimes coy,
>   Yet she never fails to please;
>   If with a Frown
>   I am cast down,
>   *Phillis* smiling,
>   And beguiling,
> Makes me happier than before.

There is only a hair's breadth between this delicious trifle and the parody that the same poet wrote of a *Song A-la-Mode*:

> O're the Desert, cross the Meadows,
>   Hunters blew the merry Horn;
> *Phoebus* chas'd the flying Shadows
>   Eccho, she reply'd, in scorn;

> Still adoring,
> And deploring;
> Why must *Thirsis* lose his Life?

In these two poems, probably written in the reign of William III, we can see, perhaps, the last appearance of the pastoral tradition as a vital element in the English lyric.

All the wits except the haughty Sheffield and the 'unspotted' Roscommon were influenced by another tradition besides that of the courtly pastoral. This was the tradition of the street ballad, that lusty growth of popular English poetry, which found expression in innumerable broadsides hawked in the streets and taverns, and in the popular anthologies like *Westminster Drollery* and *Wit's Recreation*. In the reign of Charles I certain men of letters and courtiers like Bishop Corbet and Sir John Suckling had started the fashion of writing poetry in the manner of the street ballad and the tavern song. Rochester, Sedley, Dorset and Etherege all seem to have delighted in this hearty, vigorous poetry of the common English people. Dorset is said to have collected ballads,[1] and his best poem, the 'Song', written at sea in the First Dutch War, is a true street ballad with its swinging rhythm, its full-blooded humour and its gusto. The lyrics scattered through Etherege's plays, when they are not elegant pastorals in the French manner, are snatches of song in the true popular tradition with all its sweetness and gaiety and frank enjoyment of the life of the senses:

> I gave my Love a Green-gown
> I' the merry month of *May*,
> And down she fell as wantonly,
> As a Tumbler doth at Play.

Rochester, like his contemporary Andrew Marvell, used the form as a vehicle for powerful satiric poetry. His *History of*

[1] See Addison, *Spectator*, no. 85, 7 June 1711.

Insipids is an excellent example of the popular lampoon of the Restoration with its gay, dancing rhythm, its humour and its bitter irony. That these lampoons were genuinely popular is proved by the remark of the Shoemaker in *The Man of Mode* to Dorimant (Rochester): 'Our Journeymen now adays instead of harmless Ballads, sing nothing but your damn'd Lampoons.'[1]

The Restoration Wits rendered two great services to English poetry. First they kept the singing voice of the lyric alive in an age of mathematics and scientific 'realism'. Boileau said that Descartes had cut the throat of poetry.[2] It was in a large degree due to the 'merry gang' that the mathematical spirit of Descartes and Hobbes failed to cut the throat of the English lyric. Their other valuable achievement was to produce a body of informal, unconventional verse in an age when immense prestige was enjoyed by the dignity and formality of the neo-classic manner which could easily degenerate into stiffness, pomposity and pedantry.

Congreve's enchanting heroine, Millamant, liked Suckling because he was 'natural' and 'easy'. The Restoration wits preserved the happy freedom of the 'natural, easy' tradition of English poetry which descended from Skelton, Carew, Suckling and Herrick, and which they handed on to Swift, Prior, Gay and Carey, to the Cowper of *John Gilpin* and the Byron of *Beppo* and *Don Juan*.

[1] Etherege, *Plays*, ed. Brett Smith, vol. II, p. 197.
[2] Quoted by B. Willey, *The Seventeenth Century Background*, p. 89.

Sir Charles Sedley

Sidley *has that prevailing, gentle Art,*
That can with a resistless Charm impart,
The loosest wishes to the chastest Heart.

ROCHESTER, An Allusion to Horace

Des Garnements comme Sidley.

A. HAMILTON, Mémoires de Grammont, ch. x

Sir Charles Sedley

1638–1701

THREE YOUNG MEN were dining on 16 June 1663, at 'The Cock', a tavern in Covent Garden, kept by a woman called Oxford Kate. They were Sir Charles Sedley, Lord Buckhurst and Sir Thomas Ogle. The party was possibly a celebration of the arrangements for staging a translation of a French tragedy, *La Pompée* of Corneille, to which both Sedley and Buckhurst had contributed. The dinner at Oxford Kate's developed into an orgy. After a riotous banquet, the diners went out on to the balcony of the tavern. They are said to have been 'in their shirts', but, according to one account, Sedley was entirely naked. There they performed some disgusting pranks which Pepys and Anthony à Wood describe in plain English, and Sedley, who was apt to get 'rhetorically drunk', made a speech to the onlookers which seems to have been partly a parody of a Puritan sermon and partly an imitation of a speech by a quack doctor. He ended by offering for sale a powder which would make all the women of the town run after the purchaser. By this time the crowd had swollen to about a thousand people and angry rumblings were heard. The three revellers, then 'shewing Bottles of Wine...proclaym'd, "Ho every one that thirsteth, come ye to the waters, and let him that hath no money come to buy wine and milk without money or price." '[1] After this they 'drank a health to the salvation of Judas and another to

---

[1] *The Diary and Letters of Philip Henry*, ed. M. L. See (1882), p. 158. These young men knew their Bible. Their invocation is the first verse of Isaiah lv.

the Babe of Bethlehem', and, according to Pepys, a third to the king. The infuriated mob tried to force the door of the tavern, while Sedley and his friends hurled wine bottles at them. At last the revellers, two of whom were Members of Parliament, with tipsy solemnity announced that they would 'goe in and make lawes for the nation' and quitted the balcony amid a shower of stones which smashed Oxford Kate's windows.

The Puritans naturally took full advantage of this escapade to discredit the Court, and the scandal was so great that the Government had to take action. The three young men were summoned to appear before Sir Robert Foster, Lord Chief Justice to the King's Bench. Sir Robert asked Sedley if he had read a book called *The Compleat Gentleman*, referring to the well-known work by Henry Peacham. Sedley replied rather impudently but, probably with some truth, that 'set aside his lordship he had read more books than himself'. Asked if he would stand trial at the bar, he took the sensible course of confessing the indictment and throwing himself on the mercy of the court. As ring-leader he was fined two thousand marks and imprisoned for a week. Actually one-half of the fine seems to have been remitted and Sedley paid what was in those days the considerable sum of one thousand marks (£333. 6s. 8d.).

The Sedleys or Sidleys of Southfleet were originally a Kentish family of small landowners, which, like many English families of the same class, acquired wealth and importance as a result of the social and economic changes of the sixteenth century. Sir William Sedley (1575–1619), the poet's grandfather, was a highly successful barrister, knighted in 1605 and created a baronet by James I in 1611. He was a generous patron of learning and founder of the Sedleian Lecture in Natural Philosophy in the University of Oxford. Among his friends was Sir Henry Savile, the great

Elizabethan scholar, translator of Tacitus and editor of Chrysostom. Sir William's eldest son, John, married Elizabeth Savile, Sir Henry's daughter, in 1613. Sir John and Lady Elizabeth Sedley had nine children, five of whom predeceased their father, who died in 1638. The survivors were Henry, William, Elizabeth and Charles, the poet, a posthumous child. Lady Elizabeth, the poet's mother, was a woman of high spirit, great personal charm and considerable intellectual attainments, who defended her children's interests vigorously and successfully during the troubled times of the Civil War and the Commonwealth. Edmund Waller, the poet, expressed his admiration for her in his fine 'Epitaph on the Lady Sidley':

> Here lyes the learned *Savil's* Heir
> So early wise and lasting fair;
> That none, except her years they told,
> Thought her a Child, or thought her old.

Sir Henry, Lady Elizabeth's eldest son, died in 1639, and was succeeded by his brother Sir William, a young man who, according to Anthony à Wood, lived 'very high' in London under the Protectorate. Charles Sedley entered Wadham College, Oxford, on 22 March 1655/6. He had been at Oxford for only a few weeks when his elder brother died of an attack of measles, and he inherited the title and the extensive Sedley estates. In February 1656/7, before his eighteenth birthday, he was married to Katherine Savage, a sister of his brother's wife, Lady Chandos.

After the Restoration Sir Charles is said to have 'lived mostly in the great city, became a debauchee, set up for a Satyrical wit, a comedian, poet and courtier of ladies'. He was certainly a prominent member of the group of gay young men whose company Charles II preferred to that of the old Cavaliers. Sedley was a short youth with a round face and dark eyes and was considered to resemble his grandfather, Sir Henry Savile. His nickname among the wits was 'Little Sid'. Charles II, we are told, 'delighted in him to an excess', praised his style, 'whether in Writing or Discourse', and told him on one occasion that 'Nature had given him a Patent to be *Apollo's Viceroy*'.

After the frolic at Oxford Kate's Sedley's reputation for wickedness and profanity was widespread. Pepys alludes to him in his diary with a curious mixture of horror, envy and prurient curiosity. A pious old lady called Mary Rich, Countess of Warwick, met him by chance on 5 August 1667, at Durdans, the country house of Lord Berkeley. She noted in her diary that she dined with Sedley on that day, 'which was much trouble to see him lest he should be profane. But it pleased God to restrain him; yet the knowledge I had how profane a person he is troubled me to be in his company.' Sedley had probably ridden over to Durdans from Epsom, where in July of that year, according to Pepys, he had been 'keeping merry house' with his friend Lord Buckhurst and Nell Gwyn, the pretty actress whom Buckhurst had recently persuaded to leave the stage. In these years the duke of Buckingham and the young earl of Rochester were his intimate friends. In January 1670, he was at Adderbury, the Oxfordshire estate of Rochester, and in the summer of that year he went with Buckhurst and Buckingham on a special embassy to the court of Louis XIV.

To see Sedley's character in a true perspective, it is necessary to place beside such stories as that of the notorious rag at Oxford Kate's his genuine devotion to literature and the theatre and the remarkable tributes paid to him by some of the chief contemporary men of letters. Dryden certainly had a very high opinion of Sedley both as a critic of literature and as a man. He paid him the compliment of introducing him into his *Essay of Dramatick Poesie* under the name of Lisideius,

who is one of the chief interlocutors in that celebrated critical
dialogue. It is Lisideius, or Sedley, who, 'after some modest
denials', gives the definition of what 'a play ought to be',
which is the starting point of the main argument, and Dryden
places in the mouth of the same speaker a very able and
interesting defence of French neo-classical drama. There is
no reason to doubt that the words of Lisideius are based on
memories of Sedley's conversation. Dryden also dedicated to
Sedley his comedy *The Assignation or Love in a Nunnery*
(1673). In his Dedicatory Epistle prefixed to this play he
compares the delights of evenings spent with Sedley to the
eruditam voluptatem of the ancients. 'We have, like them', he
continues, 'our genial nights, where our discourse is neither
too serious, nor too light, but always pleasant and for the
most part instructive; the raillery neither too sharp upon the
present, nor too censorious on the absent; and the cups only
such as will raise the conversation of the night without disturbing the business of the morrow.' In the same dedication
Dryden makes an interesting and significant comparison
between the popular notion of the wits as monsters of de-
bauchery and impiety and the reality of the manners of
Sedley and his friends as he knew them: 'Such wits as they
describe, I have never been so unfortunate as to meet in your
company; but have often heard much better reasoning at
your table, than I have encountered in their books. The wits
they describe, are the fops we banish: for blasphemy and
atheism, if they were neither sin nor ill manners, are subjects
so very common, and worn so threadbare, that people who
have sense avoid them. . . .' The opinion of Sedley expressed
here by Dryden is corroborated by Thomas Shadwell, the
dramatist, afterwards to become Dryden's bitter opponent.
In a dedication to Sedley of his comedy *A True Widow*,
Shadwell writes that he had heard Sedley 'speak more wit at
a supper than all my adversaries, with their heads join'd

together can write in a year'. Eighteen years later, in another dedication, Shadwell speaks of Sedley's delicacy and humanity in performing the function of a patron of men of letters: 'I shall always be proud of an occasion to boast of so good a Patron who uses me not as some Supercilious Men would (who do good merely out of vanity), as a troublesome hanger-on, but treats me with the civility and kindness of a Friend. And I have had the honour to have always found so much of both from him, as if I had obliged him in receiving as much as he did in conferring his benefits.'

The earliest record of Sir Charles's literary activities is that in the winter of 1662–3 he was collaborating with his mother's old friend, Edmund Waller, Charles Sackville, Lord Buckhurst (afterwards earl of Dorset), Sir Edward Filmer and Sidney Godolphin in a translation of Corneille's tragedy *La Mort de Pompée* into English rhyming verse. This translation, called *Pompey the Great*, was staged early in October 1663, at the Duke's Theatre. It was acted in 'English habits', and Cæsar, who appeared with 'a feather and a staff', was hissed. The citizens' wives in the audience are said to have been chiefly responsible for the failure of the production. They were probably bored by the long speeches and the lack of spectacular effects, in which Davenant's Theatre specialised.

Sedley's first original play, *The Mulberry Garden*, was produced at the King's House[1] in Drury Lane on 18 May 1668. This comedy, by one of the most prominent members of the 'merry gang' at court, aroused great expectations, but, according to Pepys, it was not very well received, and the king, who was present at the first performance, was not observed to laugh or show any sign of pleasure. The play, though it contains some excellent writing, is just what might be

---

[1] i.e. Drury Lane Theatre, so called because it was allotted to the King's Company of players.

expected from a clever young aristocratic amateur. It lacks
the two essential unities of action and atmosphere. Indeed it
looks as though it consists of two plays not very adroitly
stitched together. There are scenes in rhyming verse dealing
with the adventures of romantic figures called Eugenio,
Philander, Horatio, Diana and Althea in the last days of the
Protectorate, and other scenes in sparkling, conversational
prose obviously based on the life of the wits and ladies of the
court of Charles II. It seems likely that the serious scenes in
verse were written when Sedley was very young, perhaps
soon after the Restoration, and that the comic scenes in
prose were added to suit the taste of a public which had been
introduced by Etherege and Dryden to a new sort of comedy.

Sedley's wild life in the early years after the Restoration
may well have been due to domestic troubles. He was married
when he was a boy, and his wife, who was a Roman Catholic
(but 'far from an exemplary Catholic', we are told), became
insane after a few years of married life and had to be 'placed
under the care of a Catholic physician'. She is said to have
shown 'extreme vanity' and to have insisted on being addressed as 'Your Majesty'. At some date between 1665 and
1672 a Carmelite friar, called Father Bede, of St Simeon
Stock, was in London. He visited Lady Sedley, who was
living apart from her husband, and describes her as 'the wife
of a most eccentric English nobleman with a revenue of
twenty thousand *scudi*'. With Sir Charles's permission,
Father Bede succeeded in persuading Lady Sedley to go and
live in an English Benedictine nunnery at Ghent. This con-
vent was badly in need of money, and Sir Charles promised to
pay what was in those days the considerable sum of four
hundred pounds annually. Lady Sedley went with Father
Bede to Ghent, and lived in the Benedictine nunnery for
the rest of her life. She outlived her husband and died in
1705. Her pension was paid regularly, but was later reduced

to two hundred pounds, when the finances of the nunnery had been stabilised.

Sir Charles consoled himself with a number of temporary liaisons in the early years of the reign of Charles II. One of these was almost certainly Mary Knipp, or Napp, a lively and pretty actress at the King's House and a close ally of Nell Gwyn, with whom she acted in a number of plays. Mrs Knipp also bestowed her favours on Samuel Pepys, as readers of his diary will remember, and incurred the very natural jealousy of Mrs Pepys. Another of Sedley's mistresses, according to Pepys, was an actress at the Duke of York's Theatre called 'Pegg', 'a mighty pretty woman and seems but is not modest'. It is possible that 'Pegg' is Margaret Hughes, afterwards mistress of Prince Rupert.

At an unknown date, probably about 1670, Sedley made the acquaintance of a young woman called Anne Ayscough, daughter of Henry Ayscough, a Yorkshire gentleman. Another of his daughters, Frances Ayscough, had married Joseph Ayloffe, a distinguished barrister, with whom Sedley had some acquaintance. He probably met Anne at Ayloffe's house. He seems to have started to make love to her in his usual light-hearted manner, but he met his match in the lady and was so captivated by her beauty and her character that he ended by making her his wife in every sense except a legal one. He tells the story very frankly in his poem *To Cloris* (see p. 56).

Marriage, apparently, was the only condition on which Cloris-Anne would yield, and Sedley seems actually to have gone through a ceremony of marriage with her in April 1672. This 'marriage' was illegal and Sir Charles rendered himself liable to capital punishment for bigamy under a statute of James I. However, it must be remembered that it was impossible at that date for a commoner to obtain a divorce with permission to remarry. The only way in which such a divorce could be obtained in the seventeenth century was by a special Act of Parliament. The first 'parliamentary' divorce was that granted to Lord Roos in 1670. No commoner succeeded in obtaining a 'parliamentary' divorce before 1701. Public opinion, however, seems to have been more humane and progressive than the law, and Sedley was not only not re- garded as a bigamist, but his union with Anne Ayscough was recognised socially if not legally as a second marriage. They had two sons, the younger of whom died in childhood. The elder was named Charles after his father. He was knighted by William III and he married Frances, the daughter of Sir Richard Newdigate. The health of this young man seems to have been bad and he died in 1701 a few weeks before his father. He left a son, the third Sir Charles Sedley, who was created a baronet by Queen Anne and was the founder of a new branch of the Sedley family in Nottinghamshire.

By his legal wife Sedley had one daughter named Katherine after her mother. Katherine Sedley, a dark, thin girl with bold, sparkling eyes, was no beauty, but she inherited a good deal of her father's wit and audacity. Her childhood must have been stormy, passed as it was in a household of which the master spent his time in the taverns and theatres, and whose mistress was the mad patient of the 'Catholic physi- cian'. John Evelyn, who met her when she was only fifteen, describes her even then 'as none of the most virtuous but a wit'. Later she was the mistress of the duke of York, who, when he became King James II, created her countess of Dorchester in her own right.[1]

A change in Sir Charles's way of living was probably the result of his 'second marriage'. There seems no doubt that towards the end of the second decade of the reign of Charles II he was, in the words of Anthony à Wood, 'taking up and growing very serious'. At about this time he appears to have

[1] See below, p. 141.

moved to a house in Bloomsbury Square, then a fashionable suburban residential area. Probably he consoled himself in his retirement by turning to his books. One result of his studies was a heroic play in rhyming verse called *Antony and Cleopatra*, which was produced in February 1676/7, at the Duke's Theatre, where it had a good reception. To a modern reader this well-constructed, but vapid and ranting, play seems the least attractive of Sedley's literary productions, but it should be regarded, perhaps, as a kind of libretto for Jeremiah Clarke's music, which is said to have contributed largely to its success.

John Sheffield, earl of Mulgrave, afterwards duke of Buckinghamshire, who was at that time the bitter opponent of Rochester and his circle, attacked Sedley violently in a brutal passage in his *Essay upon Satyr*, which was circulated in manuscript in 1679:

> And little *Sid—y* for *Simile* renown'd,
> Pleasure has always sought but never found:
> Tho' all his thoughts on Wine and Women fall,
> His are so bad sure he ne're thinks at all.
> The flesh he lives upon is rank and strong,
> His meat and mistresses are kept too long;
> But sure we all mistake this Pious man
> Who mortifies his Person all he can:....[1]

The statement that Sedley's mistresses were 'kept too long' is certainly an allusion to his connection with Anne Ayscough, and the sneer at his piety to his new seriousness and interest in religion.

Sedley's favourite game was tennis, not the modern lawn tennis, but the older and more strenuous game played in a covered court. One January day in 1680 he was warming

[1] *The Fourth (and last) Collection of Poems, Satyrs, Songs, &c.* (London, 1689), p. 31. See below, pp. 219, 228.

himself by playing some sets with Etherege and Fleetwood
Shepherd in a court in Peter Street, Clare Market, when
the roof collapsed and buried the whole company in the ruins.
Both Sedley and Etherege were badly hurt. Sedley received
such severe injuries to the skull that he was at first reported
dead. According to contemporary accounts, the illness which
followed this accident had the effect of turning his thoughts
towards religion, and no doubt he was strongly affected by
the news of the conversion and death of his friend John
Wilmot, Earl of Rochester, in July 1680.

There are indications that towards the end of the reign of
Charles II Sedley joined the political opposition or 'Country
Party'. He was first elected to the House of Commons in
1688, and in 1670 was described as a 'Parliament Pensioner'
or member in receipt of payments made for support of the
court policy in the Commons. He was re-elected to the Whig
Parliaments of 1679 and 1680, and his failure to secure re-
election to the Parliament of James II in 1685 probably
indicates that he was now definitely regarded by the court as
an opponent, as the elections of 1685 were carefully manipu-
lated so as to ensure that only Tories were returned. However, he is said to have used his influence to oppose the policy
of James II, and this report is borne out by the undoubted
fact that, like his friend the Earl of Dorset, he gave his whole-
hearted support to the cause of William of Orange in 1688. It
was on this occasion that he made his most famous epigram.
Someone had found it strange that the old courtier of King
Charles should now appear as a champion of the Revolution.
Sedley answered: 'Well, I am even in point of civility with
King James. For as he made my daughter a Countess, so I
have helped to make his daughter a Queen.'

The reconstitution of Sedley's life does not seem to have
interfered with his interest in the theatre or his literary
activities. In 1687, his second comedy, *Bellamira or the*

Mistress, was staged at the King's House. This play, though founded on *The Eunuch* of Terence, is essentially an original production, a gay, witty, full-blooded comedy of Restoration life, written in racy, vigorous prose. It certainly shows that, whatever may have been the effect of Sedley's conversion, it did not turn him into a Puritan.

He sat in all the Parliaments of William III, and he has an honourable record as an outspoken, sensible, independent member. He was one of the leaders of the attack on the scandalous army of 'placemen', the disgrace of seventeenth-century Parliaments, and he made a valuable contribution to the fight for the reform of the old inhuman procedure at trials for treason. He continued to write verses and some of his most charming poems belong to the reign of William III. Several of them were contributed to *The Gentleman's Journal*, one of the earliest English literary periodicals, edited by Peter Motteux. In 1697, old Tom D'Urfey dedicated his play *The Intrigues of Versailles* to Sir Charles Sedley and his son. In this dedication he writes some words which give a pleasing picture of the relationship between the poet and the younger Sir Charles Sedley:

'There being more...than the Ordinary Duty and Love Incumbent between Father and Son, an entire, free and easie Friendship—Submission and Satisfaction on your Son's side—Contentment with Pleasure on his Father's.'

Sedley's pen was active up to the end. In 1700 he joined with a group of wits, including the young Captain Richard Steele, to reply to a ponderous attack by Sir Richard Blackmore, the physician-poet, and in the following year he contributed his fine version of a famous ode of Horace to a miscellany edited by Charles Gildon. At the end of May 1701, the younger Sedley died at the age of twenty-nine. His father did not long survive him. He was seriously ill in July, but had somewhat recovered by the beginning of August. On the advice of Sir Hans Sloane he moved to a cottage at Hampstead. After spending three weeks there, he died at the end of August, and it is pleasant to learn from an eye-witness that he met death 'like a philosopher without fear or superstition'. In the following year the bookseller John Nutt published Sedley's long poem on matrimony called *The Happy Pair* and his *Miscellaneous Works* edited by Captain William Ayloffe, a nephew of Anne Ayscough.

Sedley is not a great poet, but he is a genuine poet of a kind that no longer exists. He is a gentleman-amateur, but not a dilettante or a mere dabbler in elegant pastiche. His poems grow directly out of his life and are a natural product of the society in which he lived. Pope said that 'Sedley was an insipid poet except in a few of his little love verses'. This is not quite fair to Sedley, who wrote some good poetry besides his 'little love verses', though these are certainly his most notable poems. They belong to the old courtly convention of love-making which was still a reality at the court of Charles II. According to this convention the lady was a fortress which the lover attacked with certain recognised weapons, among which verses were considered to be particularly deadly and effective. In Dangerfield's song in *Bellamira* (see p. 58) the lover's offensive weapons are enumerated. They are oaths, *billets-doux*, songs and 'amorous stories'. According to the rules of the game the lady had to defend her 'honour' and the lover had to persuade her that the religion of 'honour' was a false one.

> Why shou'd this Tyrant Honour make
> Our cruel undeserved Wrack?

> Come then, my *Celia*, let's no more
> This Devil for a God adore.

The typical situation is that in which the lover (or 'shepherd') tries to induce the lady (or 'nymph') to come and live with him in a pagan dream-world where there are no inhibitions and the law is the *fays ce que vouldras* of the Abbey of Theleme. It is with reference to this convention that we must read the playful lines which Rochester wrote on his friend in his *Allusion to Horace*:

> *Sidley* has that prevailing gentle Art,
> That can with a resistless Charm impart,
> The loosest wishes, to the chastest Heart,
> Raise such a conflict, kindle such a *Fire*,
> Betwixt declining *Virtue* and *Desire*,
> Till the poor vanquisht *Maid* dissolves away
> In *Dreams* all *Night*, in *Sighs* and *Tears* all Day.

These lines were absurdly interpreted by late writers as meaning that Sedley is a licentious and voluptuous writer. All that Rochester means is that he played the traditional game gracefully and successfully, and that his verses helped him in his conquests. Occasionally he assumes a cynical pose, but he is not really a wild bohemian or a bacchanalian poet. His one drinking song is rather half-hearted:

> Drink about till the Day find us;
>   These are Pleasures that will last;
> Let no foolish Passion blind us,
>   Joys of Love they fly too fast.

Some of his best lyrics are the result of his enjoyment of the courtly-love game, which he plays with a mixture of easy grace and a certain rather attractive boyish clumsiness. He has a gift for verbal melody and he is most successful when he uses it to express his sheer æsthetic pleasure in the situations arising from convention of gallantry:

> Hears not my *Phillis*, how the Birds
> Their feather'd Mates salute?
> They tell their Passion in their Words;
> Must I alone be mute?
> Phillis, *without Frown or Smile*,
> *Sat and knotted all the while.*

It is a charming game, but Sedley's real ideal, like that of many libertines, is the tranquillity of a happy marriage of true minds, expressed with such touching simplicity in his one great love song:

> All that in Woman is ador'd
> In thy dear Self I find,
> For the whole sex can but afford,
> The Handsome and the Kind.

Sedley is not exclusively, however, what Ben Jonson calls a 'women's poet'. There is a more masculine and intellectual note in some of his later verses. *The Physician and his Patients* is an excellent little ironic fable worthy of Swift in his lighter moods, and the version of Horace's Ode to Barine is a splendid piece of work, strong, vivid and as firmly built as the Latin original. T. E. Page considered it to be the 'only adequate English rendering' of any ode of Horace. It was probably of this poem that Prior was thinking when he declared that Sir Charles 'could write, but better translate'. The adaptations of a series of epigrams of Martial under the title of 'Court Characters', probably written late in life, suggest that he might have succeeded as a satiric commentator on the contemporary scene. One of the characters ('To Quintus'), written in what was then the uncommon form of the Shakespearian sonnet, is an incisive criticism of the life of the sensualist, which we should hardly expect from the hero of the rag at Oxford Kate's. *The Happy Pair* is a powerful social commentary in verse, in which the poet, obviously drawing on his own experience, bitterly denounces the loveless and mercenary marriages of his class. The conclusion of this poem with its praise of quiet domesticity shows that the wild gallant of the sixties had developed by the end of the century into an Augustan gentleman, almost into a Man of Feeling. When these lines were written the Restoration Carnival was over and the age when an 'ounce of feeling' was preferred to 'a pound of fancy' was in sight.

Many of Sedley's lyrics were first printed in 1672 in a volume published by Hobart Kemp called *A Collection of Poems Written Upon Several Occasions by Several Persons*. Revised versions of most of these poems appeared in the collected edition of Sedley's *Miscellaneous Works* (1702), edited by Captain William Ayloffe, the nephew of Anne Ayscough. In the following selection I have generally given the poems in the text of the 1702 edition, as I believe they represent the author's latest revisions. I have, however, printed the earlier version of the lines *To Cloris* (see p. 56), because it has a biographical interest which is considerably diminished in the revised text, where the final couplet is omitted. The songs from the plays were not reprinted by Ayloffe; the versions given here are those which appeared in the original quarto editions. Where no source is indicated at the foot of a poem, the text is that of the *Miscellaneous Works* of 1702.

Poems by Sir Charles Sedley

SONG

Phillis, let's shun the common Fate,
And let our Love ne'r turn to Hate;
I'll dote no longer then I can,
Without being call'd a faithless Man.
When we begin to want Discourse,
And Kindness seems to tast of Force,
As freely as we met, we'll part,
Each one possest of their own Heart.
Thus whilst rash Fools themselves undo;
We'll Game and give off Savers too;*
So equally the match we'll make,
Both shall be glad to draw the Stake:
A Smile of thine shall make my Bliss,
I will enjoy thee in a Kiss;
If from this Height our Kindness fall,
We'll bravely scorn to Love at all:
If thy Affection first decay,
I will the Blame on Nature lay.
Alas, what Cordial can remove
The hasty Fate of dying Love?
Thus we will all the world excel
In Loving, and in Parting well.

---

10 ...*Savers too*. This is a metaphor from cards or dice. *Game*=play; *Give off*=give over, cease playing; *Savers*=one who escapes loss without gain (Johnson).

SONG

Ah *Cloris!* that I now could sit
   As unconcern'd as when
Your Infant Beauty cou'd beget
   No pleasure, nor no pain.

When I the Dawn us'd to admire,
   And prais'd the coming day;
I little thought the growing fire
   Must take my Rest away.

Your charms in harmless Childhood lay,
   Like metals in the mine,
Age from no face took more away,
   Than Youth conceal'd in thine.

But as your Charms insensibly
   To their perfection prest,
Fond Love as unperceiv'd did flye,
   And in my Bosom rest.

My passion with your Beauty grew,
   And *Cupid* at my heart,
Still as his mother favour'd you,
   Threw a new flaming Dart.

Each glori'd in their wanton part,
   To make a Lover he
Employ'd the utmost of his Art,
   To make a Beauty she.

Though now I slowly bend to love,
   Uncertain of my Fate,
If your fair self my Chains approve,
   I shall my freedom hate.

Lovers, like dying men, may well
   At first disorder'd be,
Since none alive can truly tell
   What Fortune they must see.

From The Mulberry Garden, 1668,
Act III, sc. ii

SONG

Phillis is my only Joy,
   Faithless as the Winds or Seas;
Sometimes coming, sometimes coy,
   Yet she never fails to please;
     If with a Frown
     I am cast down,
     Phillis smiling,
     And beguiling,
Makes me happier than before.

Tho', alas, too late I find,
   Nothing can her Fancy fix;
Yet the moment she is kind,
   I forgive her all her Tricks;
     Which, tho' I see,
     I can't get free;
     She deceiving,
     I believing;
What can Lovers wish for more?

TO CELIA

You tell me, *Celia*, you approve,
Yet never must return my Love:
And Answer that my Hope Destroys,
And in the Cradle wounds our Joys;
To kill at once what needs must die,
None would to Birds and Beasts deny.
How can you then so Cruel prove,
As to preserve, and torture Love?
That Beauty Nature kindly meant
For her own Pride, and our Content;
Why shou'd the Tyrant Honour make
Our cruel undeserved Wrack?
In Love and War th' Impostor do's
The Best to greatest Harms expose:
Come then, my *Celia*, let's no more
This Devil for a God adore;
Like foolish *Indians* we have been,
Whose whole Religion is a Sin:
Let's lose no Time then but repent,
Love welcomes best a Penitent.

HER ANSWER

Thirsis, I wish, as well as you,
To Honour there were nothing due,
Then would I pay my Debt of Love
In the same Coin that you approve;
Which now you must in Friendship take,
'Tis all the payment I can make;
Friendship so high that I must say,
'Tis rather Love, with some Allay;
And rest contented, since that I
As well my self as you deny.
Learn then of me, bravely to bear,
The want of that you hold most dear;
And that which Honour does in me,
Let my Example work in thee.

TO AMARANTA

Whom he fell in love with at a Playhouse

Fair *Amaranta* on the Stage, whilst you
Pitty'd a feigned Love, you gave a true;
The Hopes and Fears, in every Scene exprest,
Grew soon th' uneasie Motions of my Breast.
I thought to steal the innocent Delight,
And not have paid my Heart for a first Sight.
And if I ventur'd on some slight Discourse,
It should be such as could no Passion nurse:
Led by the treacherous Lustre of your Eyes,
At last I play'd too near the Precipice:
Love came disguis'd in Wonder and Delight,
His Bow unbent, his Arrows out of sight;
Your Words fell on my Passion, like those Showers,
Which paint and multiply the rising Flowers;
Like *Cupid's* self, a God, and yet a Child,
Your Looks at once were awful, and yet mild:
Methoughts you blush'd, as conscious of my Flame,
Whilst your strict Vertue did your Beauty blame:
But rest secure, y'are from the Guilt as free
As Saints ador'd from our Idolatry.

TO A DEVOUT YOUNG GENTLEWOMAN

Phillis, this early Zeal asswage,
   You over-act your part;
The Martyrs, at your tender Age,
   Gave Heaven but half their Heart.

Old Men (till past the Pleasure) ne're
   Declaim against the Sin;
'Tis early to begin to fear
   The Devil at Fifteen.

The World to Youth is too severe,
   And, like a treacherous Light,
Beauty the Actions of the Fair,
   Exposes to their sight.

And yet this World, as old as 'tis,
   Is oft deceiv'd by't too;
Kind Combinations seldom miss,
   Let's try what we can do.

SONG

Love still has somthing of the Sea,
  From whence his Mother rose;
No time his Slaves from Doubt can free,
  Nor give their Thoughts repose:

They are becalm'd in clearest Days,
  And in rough Weather tost;
They wither under cold Delays,
  Or are in Tempests lost.

One while they seem to touch the Port,
  Then straight into the Main,
Some angry Wind in cruel sport
  The Vessel drives again.

At first Disdain and Pride they fear,
  Which if they chance to 'scape,
Rivals and Falshood soon appear
  In a more dreadful shape.

By such Degrees to Joy they come,
  And are so long withstood,
So slowly they receive the Sum,
  It hardly does them good.

'Tis cruel to prolong a Pain,
  And to defer a Joy;
Believe me, gentle *Celemene*,
  Offends the winged Boy.

An hundred thousand Oaths your Fears
  Perhaps would not remove;
And if I gaz'd a thousand Years
  I could no deeper love.

SONG

Get you gone, you will undo me,
If you love me, don't pursue me,
Let that Inclination perish,
Which I dare no longer cherish;
With harmless Thoughts I did begin,
But in the Crowd Love entred in;
I knew him not, he was so gay,
So innocent and full of Play;
At every Hour in every Place,
I either saw or form'd your Face;
All that in Plays was finely writ,
Fancy for you, and me did fit.
My Dreams at Night were all of you,
Such as till then I never knew:
I sported thus with young Desire,
Never intending to go higher:
But now his Teeth and Claws are grown,
Let me the fatal Lion shun;
You found me harmless, leave me so;
For were I not, you'd leave me too.

SONG

Walking among thick Shades alone,
  I heard a distant Voice,
Which, sighing, said, Now she is gone,
  I'll make no second Choice.

I look't and saw it was a Swain,
  Who to the flying Wind,
Did of some neighbouring Nymph complain,
  Too fair, and too unkind.

He told me how he saw her first,
  And with what gracious Eyes,
And gentle Speech, that Flame she nurst,
  Which since she did despise.

His Vows she did as fast receive,
  As he could breathe 'em to her;
Love in her Eyes proclaim'd her leave,
  That he alone should woo her.

They fed their Flocks still near one Place,
  And at one instant met,
He gazing on her lovely Face
  Fell deeper in the Net.

She seem'd of her new Captive glad;
  Proud of his Bondage he,
No lover, sure a Prospect had
  Of more Felicity.

But the false Maid, or never lov'd,
  Or gave so quickly o're;
E're his was to the height improv'd,
  Her Kindness was no more.

Even her Dissemblings she let fall,
  And made him plainly see,
That though his Heart she did enthral,
  Her own was ever free.

Now, lest his care should Pity move,
  She shuns his very Sight;
And leaves him to that hopeless Love,
  She did create in Spight.

Her name I could not make him tell,
  Though vowing him my aid;
He said he never would reveal,
  In Life, nor Death, the Maid.

SONG A-LA-MODE

O're the Desert, cross the Meadows,
  Hunters blew the merry Horn;
Phoebus chas'd the flying Shadows:
  Eccho, she reply'd in scorn;
    Still adoring,
    And deploring:
Why must *Thirsis* lose his life?

Rivers murmur'd from their Fountains,
  Acorns dropping from their Oaks,
Fawns came tripping o're the Mountains,
  Fishes bit the naked Hooks;
    Still admiring,
    And desiring:
When shall *Phillis* be a Wife?

TO CLORIS

Cloris, I justly am betray'd
By a design my self had laid,
Like an old Rook,* whom in his cheat
A run of Fortune does defeat.
I thought at first with a small sum
Of love, thy heap to overcome;
Presuming on thy want of art,
Thy gentle and unpractis'd heart.
But naked Beauty can prevail,
Like open force, when plots do fail.
Instead of that thou hast all mine,
And I have not one stake of thine:
And, like all winners, do'st discover
A willingness to give me over.
And though I beg, thou wilt not now;
'Twere better thou should'st do so too;
For I so far in debt shall run,
Even thee I shall be forc't to shun.
My hand, alas, is no more mine,
Else it had long ago been thine.
My heart I give thee, and we call
No man unjust who parts with all.
What a Priest says moves not the mind,
Souls are by love, not words, combin'd.

From *A Collection of Poems written upon
Several Occasions by Several Persons*, 1672

3 *Rook* = sharper.

THE EIGHTH ODE OF THE SECOND BOOK OF HORACE

Did any Punishment attend
    Thy former Perjuries,
I should believe a second Time,
    Thy charming Flatteries:
Did but one Wrinkle mark this Face,
Or hadst thou lost one single Grace.

No sooner hast thou, with false Vows,
    Provok'd the Powers above;
But thou art fairer than before,
    And we are more in love.
Thus Heaven and Earth seem to declare,
They pardon Falshood in the Fair.

Sure 'tis no Crime vainly to swear,
    By every Power on high,
And call our bury'd Mother's Ghost
    A Witness to the Lye:
Heaven at such Perjury connives,
And *Venus* with a smile forgives.

The Nymphs and cruel *Cupid* too,
    Sharp'ning his pointed Dart
On an old Hone, besmear'd with Blood,
    Forbear thy perjur'd Heart.
Fresh Youth grows up, to wear thy Chains,
And the old Slave no Freedom gains.

Thee, Mothers for their eldest Sons,
    Thee, wretched Misers fear,
Lest thy prevailing Beauty should
    Seduce the hopeful Heir:
New-marry'd Virgins fear thy Charms
Should keep their Bridegrooms from their Arms.

DANGERFIELD'S SONG

When first I made Love to my *Cloris*,
Cannon Oaths I brought down
To batter the Town,
And I fir'd her with Amorous Stories.

Billet Doux like small Shot did ply her,
And sometimes a Song
Went whizzing along,
But still I was never the nigher.

At last she sent Word by a Trumpet,
If I lik'd that Life
She wou'd be my Wife,
But never be any Man's Strumpet.

I told her that *Mars* wou'd not Marry,
And Swore by my Scars,
Single Combats, and Wars,
I'de rather Dig Stones in a Quarry.

From *Bellamira, or The Mistress,*
A Comedy, 1687, Act III, sc. i

SONG

Thyrsis unjustly you Complain,
  And tax my tender heart
With want of pity for your pain,
  Or Sense of your desert.

By secret and Mysterious Springs,
  Alas! our Passions move;
We Women are Fantastick things,
  That like before we love.

You may be handsome, and have Wit,
  Be secret and well-bred,
That Person Love must to us fit,
  He only can succeed.

Some Dye, yet never are believ'd;
  Others we trust too soon,
Helping our selves to be deceiv'd,
  And proud to be undone.

From Bellamira, or The Mistress,
A Comedy, 1687, Act III, sc. iii

SONG

Hears not my *Phillis*, how the Birds
   Their feather'd Mates salute?
They tell their Passion in their Words;
   Must I alone be mute?
Phillis, *without Frown or Smile,*
Sat and knotted all the while.

The God of Love in thy bright Eyes
   Does like a Tyrant reign;
But in thy Heart a Child he lyes,
   Without his Dart or Flame.
Phillis, *without Frown or Smile,*
Sat and knotted all the while.

So many Months in Silence past,
   And yet in raging Love,
Might well deserve one Word at last
   My Passion shou'd approve.
Phillis, *without Frown or Smile,*
Sat and knotted all the while.

Must then your faithful Swain expire,
   And not one Look obtain,
Which he to sooth his fond Desire,
   Might pleasingly explain?
Phillis, *without Frown or Smile,*
Sat and knotted all the while.

A DIALOGUE

MARS   *Cupid,* I hear thou hast improv'd
        Thy little Art of War;
    Old Men conceit they may be lov'd,
        And Cripples win the Fair.

    False powder'd Beaux at distance kill,
        And every Fop writes Songs;
    Musick imploys her utmost Skill,
        And to thy Camp belongs.

CUPID   Great God of War, why shou'd not I
        As well as you advance,
    And by new Ways make Lovers dye,
        While you bomb Towns in *France*.

    William and *Louis* are your Pride,
        *Belle Dives,** and *Stowel** mine,
    Whose Batteries Men can less abide
        Than those upon the *Rhine*.

14 *Belle Dives:* Annabella Dives or Dive, daughter of John Dive, Clerk of the Council. She was a maid of honour to Mary II and married Sir R. Howard in February 1692/3. *Stowel:* Lady Margaret Stowell, daughter of the third Earl of Salisbury, who married Lord Stowell about May 1691.

THE DOCTOR AND HIS PATIENTS

There was a prudent grave Physician,
Careful of Patients as you'd wish one;
Much good he did with Purge and Glister,
And well he knew to raise a Blister;
Many he cur'd and more he wou'd,
By Vomit, Flux and letting Blood;
But still his Patients came again,
And most of their old Ills complain;
The Drunkards drank, and spoil'd their Liver:
Beaux ply'd the Smock as much as ever,
And got the high Veneral Feaver:
The Glutton cram'd at noon and Supper,
And doubled both his Paunch and Crupper.

One Day he call'd 'em all together,
And one by one, he askt 'em whether
It were not better by good Diet,
To keep their Blood and Humours quiet;
With Tost and Ale to cool their Brains,
Than nightly Fire 'em with *Champains*;
To sup sometimes on Water-grewel,
Than drink themselves into a Duel;
To change their lewd for sober Life,
And rotten Whore, for Sounder Wife:
They all agreed that his Advice
Was honest, wholsom, grave and wise;
But not one Man, wou'd quit his Vice;
For after all his vain Attacks,
They rose and din'd well at *Pontack's*:*

The Moral
*The Wise may preach, and Satyrists rail,
Custom and Nature will prevail.*

28 *Pontack's:* a celebrated French restaurant in Abchurch Lane.

A BALLAD

To the Tune of Bateman

You Gallants all, that love good Wine,
    For shame your Lives amend;
With Strangers go to Church, or Dine,
    But drink with an old Friend.

For with him tippling all the Night,
    You kiss, hugg, and embrace;
Whereas a Stranger, at first sight,
    May kill you on the Place.

There was a rich old Usurer,
    A gallant Son he had;
Who slew an ancient Barrister,
    Like a true mettled Lad.

All in that very House where Saint
    Holds Devil by the Nose;
These Drunkards met to Roar, and Rant,
    But quarrell'd in the close.

The Glass flew chearfully about,
    And drunken Chat went on;
Which Troops had fail'd, and which were stout,
    When *Namur* wou'd be won.

A learned Lawyer, at the last,
    No Tory, as I'm told,
Began to talk of Tyrants past,
    In Words both sharp and bold.

He toucht a little on our Times,
    Defin'd the Power of Kings,
What were their Vertues, what their Crimes,
    And many dangerous Things.

A Stranger that sat Silent by,
    And scarce knew what he meant,
O're come with Wine and Loyalty,
    Did thus his Passion vent:

I cannot bear the least ill Word,
    That lessens any King;
And that bold Man shall feel my Sword;
    At that their Friends stept in.

The Quarrel seem'd a while compos'd,
    And many Healths there past,
But one to Blood was ill dispos'd,
    As it appear'd at last.

The Counsellor was walking Home,
    Sober, as he was wont,
The young man after him did come,
    With Sword, that was not blunt.

A Blow there past, which no Man saw,
    From Cane of Lawyer bold;
The young Man did his Weapon draw,
    And left the Lawyer cold.

Which Cane held up, in his Defence,
    Was judg'd a Weapon drawn:
What needs there farther Evidence,
    Th' Assault was very plain.

At *Hixes's* Hall, by Jury grave,
    It was Man-slaughter found;
O what wou'd it have cost to have
    A Pardon from the Crown.

Then learn, my honest Country-men,
    To take yourselves the Pence;

Wisely prevent the Courtier's Gain,
    And save us the Expence.

You Gallants all, take heed how you
    Come to untimely Ends;
Justice has bid the World adieu,
    And dead Men have no Friends.

This poem, in the style of the popular journalistic street ballad, describes the killing of a barrister called John Hoyle by a young man called George Pitts in the small hours of Friday, 27 May 1692, after the two men had quarrelled in the Young Devil Tavern in Fleet Street. Pitts was tried at the Old Bailey in June 1692 and found guilty of manslaughter. He 'petitioned the benefit of his clergy' and was pardoned (see ll. 53-6).

TO SEXTUS

From Martial, Lib. 2, Ep. 38

What Business, or what Hope brings thee to Town,
    Who can'st not Pimp, nor Cheat, nor Swear nor Lye?
This Place will nourish no such idle Drone;
    Hence, in remoter Parts thy Fortune try.
But thou hast Courage, Honesty, and Wit,
    And one, or all these three, will give thee Bread:
The Malice of this Town thou know'st not yet;
    Wit is a good Diversion, but base Trade;
Cowards will, for thy Courage, call thee Bully,
    Till all, like *Thraso's*, thy Acquaintance shun;
Rogues call thee for thy Honesty a Cully;
    Yet this is all thou has to live upon:
Friend, three such Vertues, *Audley** had undone;
Be wise, and e're th' art in a Jayl, be gone,
Of all that starving Crew we saw to Day
None but has kill'd his Man, or writ his Play.

13 *Audley:* Hugh Audley, a famous usurer who died on 15 November 1662
worth £400,000.

TO QUINTUS

Thou art an Atheist, *Quintus*, and a Wit,
    Thinkst all was of self-moving Attoms made,
Religion only for the Vulgar fit,
    Priests Rogues, and Preaching their deceitful Trade;
Wilt drink, whore, fight, blaspheme, damn, curse and swear:
    Why wilt thou swear, by God, if there be none?
And if there be, thou shou'd'st his Vengeance fear;
    Methinks this Huffing might be let alone;
'Tis thou art free, Mankind besides a Slave,
    And yet a Whore may lead thee by the Nose
A drunken Bottle, and a flatt'ring Knave,
    A mighty Prince, Slave to thy dear Soul's Foes,
Thy Lust, thy Rage, Ambition and thy Pride;
He that serves God, need nothing serve beside.

FROM
'THE HAPPY PAIR'

I

Both Sexes now deprave their Noble Kind,
While sordid Avarice corrupts the Mind.
Never consult poor Vertue when they choose.
But for a painted Cloud, the Goddess loose.
Divine content they count a finer Cheat,
A Dish for Ornament, but no true Meat....
With palpitations of Regret they Twine,
Like Oil and Water their false Loves combine.
With feign'd Embrace they seem Love's Joys to crave,
But with their Bed, converted to a Grave:
And whilst their backward Hearts like Load-stones meet,
They wish their Linnen were their Winding-sheet.
He, like the Bear of Love, her Body Clips,
Instead of pressing, bites her glowing Lips.
She, like a wounded *Otter*, flings and Rails,
Fires with her Tongue and combats with her Nails.
Hell and Confusion seize the Place around,
Nothing but mutual Frenzy's to be found.
They both launch out into a Sea of Strife,
A clam'rous Husband, and a Brawling Wife.

II

Love, like a cautious fearful Bird, ne'er builds,
But where the Place Silence and Calmness yields:
He slily flies to Copses, where he finds
The snugging Woods secure from Blasts and Winds,
Shuns the huge Boughs of a more Stately Form,
And Laughs at Trees tore up with ev'ry Storm.
The pleasant Nightingale can ne'er be won,
To quit a Temp'rate Shade, to scorch i' th' Sun;
In some low Grove, he sings his Charming Note,
And on a Thorn tunes the sweet Warbling Throat.

We'll take a Rustick Couple for our Scenes,
Who love but know not what Ambition means:
Who such an even competence possess,
What may support, but not disturb their Bliss.
See how unmov'd they at all Changes stand,
Shipwrecks at Sea, and Earthquakes on the Land:
The Fraud of Courts, the Knavish Toil of Clowns,
A Monarch's Favour, or his pointed Frowns....
Here let 'em live to share all Wealth and Pow'r,
As Greatness can't love less, they can't love more,
To the Divinest State of things they drive,
Like Pilgrim-Angels, on the Earth they live,
Kind Nature gave them, Fortune bore no part,
Love join'd their Souls, and Heav'n seal'd each Heart.

From *The Happy Pair: Or A Poem on Matrimony*, 1702

SONG

Not *Celia*, that I juster am
    Or better than the rest,
For I would change each Hour like them,
    Were not my Heart at rest.

But I am ty'd to very thee,
    By every Thought I have,
Thy Face I only care to see,
    Thy Heart I only crave.

All that in Woman is ador'd,
    In thy dear Self I find,
For the whole Sex can but afford,
    The Handsome and the Kind.

Why then should I seek farther Store,
    And still make Love a-new;
When Change itself can give no more,
    'Tis easie to be true.

Sir George Etherege

Dominus Etherege...homo vulgatae nequitiae, et ad usum omnium facinorum peritissimus.

Letter from H. HUGHES to the
Chamberlains of Ratisbon

That profligate coxcomb Sir George Etherege.

LORD MACAULAY, *History of England*, ch. VIII

Sir George Etherege
1635?–1691

IN MARCH 1664, a new comedy, entitled *The Comical Revenge or Love in a Tub*, was staged at the Duke's Theatre in Lincoln's Inn Fields. The cast included some of the best actors and actresses of the day, such as Thomas Betterton and his wife, Harris, Nokes and Mrs Davies, and the play had a resounding success. It is said to have brought a thousand pounds to the company in a month and to have 'gained more reputation than any previous comedy'. It was written by a slender, fair young man called George Etherege, who had been an apprentice to an attorney. He was the grandson of George Etherege of Maidenhead, Berkshire, a vintner, who was one of the original adventurers of the Bermuda Company. The vintner's son, Captain George Etherege, lived for some time in the Bermudas, and, on his return to England, bought a place at the court of Charles I. This Captain George Etherege died in 1649 in France, whither he had probably followed the exiled court after the collapse of the Royalist armies. His son George was born in 1635 at Maidenhead, probably in his grandfather's house, and it is likely that he received his early education with his father in France. He was in England in 1653, when his grandfather apprenticed him to Mr Gosnell, a London attorney. What happened to him in the eleven years between this date and the production of *The Comical Revenge* is unknown, but something can be divined from the play.

The Comical Revenge is an extremely clever but immature performance. It contains some admirable writing, but lacks unity. There are no fewer than four plots, one serious and three comic. The serious action is unfolded in scenes written in smooth, rhyming verse, and it deals with the adventures of aristocrats called Lord Beaufort, Captain Bruce, Lovis, Aurelia and Graciana. One of the three comic plots is in the manner of the old English comedy of the tavern and the street; it shows us the 'bubbling' of the absurd gull, Sir Nicholas Cully, one of 'Oliver's Knights' by the sharpers Wheadle and Palmer, who swindle their victim out of a thousand pounds and nearly succeed in inveigling him into marrying a prostitute called Grace. However, one can forgive Palmer much for the joyous snatches of song which he is constantly trolling. These scenes show a knowledge of the old English drama, together with an observation of the seamy side of London life which would come naturally enough to a sharp young lawyer's clerk in the last years of the Protectorate and the early years of the reign of Charles II. The second comic plot, which gives the play its title, deals with the adventures of the French valet Dufoy. The admirable speech (singled out for praise by Coleridge) in which Dufoy tells how he met his future master near the Pont Neuf shows a knowledge of Parisian life and character which suggests that the young Etherege had lived in France and had used his eyes and ears to good purpose. The third comic plot is the most significant of all. It is concerned with the exploits of Sir Frederick Frollick, Dufoy's master, a young spark who leads a gay life with his rude, ranting companions, waging 'bloody war with the constable', committing 'a general massacre on the glass windows', courting a rich widow, kissing her maids and performing his wild pranks with such an easy grace that no one can be really angry with him. Sir Frederick is only a sketch, but he is a sketch of genius, the first appearance on the stage of the witty, handsome rake of quality who was to be the central figure of the new comedy of wit and conversation. Dryden, in his *Wild Gallant* (1663), had made a clumsy attempt to portray such a character, but the only interesting part of that comedy is its title. The attorney's clerk succeeded where the professional poet failed. In Sir Frederick he has brought the typical Wild Gallant of the Restoration to life in English comedy. How did he do it? A little light on this subject is thrown by the dedication of the play to Charles Sackville, Lord Buckhurst: 'The Writing of it [the play] was a means to make me known to your Lordship; The Acting of it has lost me no Reputation; and the Printing of it has now given me an opportunity to show how much I honour you. I here dedicate it, as I have long since dedicated my self, to your Lordship.' These words show that Etherege had been on intimate terms for some time with Buckhurst, one of the most brilliant figures among the literary courtiers, and that it was through the writing of *The Comical Revenge* that he had made his acquaintance. The attorney's clerk had doubtless been an admiring spectator of the exploits of the 'merry gang' and the writing of his play secured his admission to the society that met at 'The Rose' 'The Dog and Partridge', and Oxford Kate's. Gentle George or Easy Etherege, as the dramatist was nicknamed among the wits, had seen Sir Frederick at close quarters in the persons of men like Buckhurst, Sedley and Savile.

On 6 February 1667/8, Gentle George appeared again before the public as the author of a comedy. His second play, *She wou'd if she cou'd*, was produced on this date at the Duke's Theatre with a cast almost as strong as that which had such a success in *The Comical Revenge*. Like Sedley's *The Mulberry Garden* in the following May, *She wou'd if she cou'd* aroused great expectations. The Duke's House was crowded with fashionable people at the first performance. The king was there, and in the pit the great George Villiers, duke of Buckingham, who had recently killed the earl of

Shrewsbury in a duel, sat 'openly' with Buckhurst, Sedley and Etherege himself. According to Samuel Pepys, the crowd was so great that a thousand people were turned away from the pit and he and his wife managed with difficulty to get seats in the '18*d.* box'. The audience, however, was disappointed. The actors were 'out of humour' and did not know their parts, and Pepys heard Etherege 'mightily find fault' with them. Pepys tells us that the audience 'blamed the play as a silly dull thing, though there was something very roguish and witty; but the design of the play, and end, mighty insipid'.

The failure of the first performance was, however, to some extent redeemed by later productions and the best critics did not agree with Pepys's sweeping condemnation. Shadwell, for instance, in the Preface to *The Humorists* (1671), roundly declared it to be 'the best Comedy since the Restauration of the Stage'. Although it does not contain any single character as entertaining as Sir Frederick Frollick, it is certainly a better play than *The Comical Revenge*. The heroic scenes in rhyming verse have disappeared and so has the low comedy of the sharpers and gulls of the London taverns. The plot is slight enough, but there is an admirable unity of tone and atmosphere. It is a sparkling picture of the life of the town as Etherege knew it. Courtal and Freeman are idle, attractive young sparks who 'follow the old trade; eat well', and prepare themselves 'with a Bottle or two of good *Burgundy*'. Sir Oliver Cockwood and his friend Sir Joslin Jolly are slightly ridiculous country knights, greedy for the pleasures of the town after a long fast in the backwoods; but the cream of the play is to be found in Ariana and Gatty, Sir Joslin's young kinswomen, two delightfully fresh and graceful girls, 'country fillies that have been breath'd at Course a Park, and Barly Break', yet armed with a keen wit which makes them worthy opponents of the young gallants

Unlike his friends Buckingham, Rochester, Buckhurst and Sedley, Etherege had not inherited a great estate, and to live in the company of the choice spirits of Whitehall and Covent Garden must have been an expensive matter. It was certainly impossible to live the life of a gentleman in that set on the proceeds of two comedies, however successful they may have been. Somebody in a high place (it is pleasant to think it may have been King Charles II) had the wit to offer Sir George a diplomatic appointment. This was probably the first time that an English writer had been rewarded in this way, and a precedent was established which was to lead to interesting results in the Augustan age. Etherege accepted the offer, and in August 1668, went to Constantinople as Secretary to Sir Daniel Harvey, who had succeeded the earl of Winchilsea as 'Ambassador Extraordinary from his Majesty into Turkey'. One of his official letters from Constantinople, dated 3 May 1670, has survived. It is an admirable piece of writing, and it has been said that 'a better informed or better written document does not exist in all the Turkey State Papers'. It contains shrewd and penetrating descriptions of the 'Grand Signor' (the Sultan), his favourite, and the Vizir Kara Mustafa. There is a vivid thumbnail sketch of the Sultana worthy of the author of *The Comical Revenge* and *She wou'd if she cou'd*. 'The Sultana is a Candiot, and though women here are not so polite & refin'd as in Christendome, yet she wants not her little arts to secure her Sultan's affections; she can dissemble fondness & jealousy, and can swoone at pleasure.'

In July Etherege seems to have been at Belgrade with Harvey, who mentions in a letter from that city that Etherege was ill. Possibly his illness was the cause of his return to England. We hear of him in Paris on May Day, 1671; in the autumn of that year he was back in London and John Muddiman, the news-letter writer, in a letter to the earl of

Rochester, mentions a scuffle in Covent Garden in which he was involved: 'This side [of the page] shall carry you within the rayles of Covent Garden where you shall behold the furious combat of Ashton and Etherege, which ended happily in a fall on Ashton's part—company interposing and not suffering him to renew fight.'

Gentle George seems to have renewed his relations with the theatre soon after his return. In November the Duke's company opened at their new playhouse in Dorset Garden with Dryden's *Sir Martin Mar-All*, and Etherege wrote a special prologue for the occasion. In 1672 a number of his lyrics and occasional poems appeared in Hobart Kemp's *A Collection of Poems* together with verses by Sedley and Buckhurst. Rochester, in an amusing passage in his *Timon*, a satire probably written about his time, gently rallies Etherege on these productions and also on his first two comedies. It is true that the passage is placed in the mouth of an absurd person called Dingboy, who is discussing contemporary authors after dinner with his friends Halfwit, Huffe and Kickum, but the criticism of the comedies as 'talking plays' is shrewd enough:

> Damn me (says *Dingboy*) in my mind, *God-swounds*,
> E[therege] writes *Airy Songs*, and soft *Lampoons*,
> The best of any *Man*; as for your *Nowns*,
> *Grammar*, and Rules *of Art*, he knows 'em not,
> Yet writ two talking *Plays* without one *Plot*.

It was not until 1676 that Gentle George produced his third play. His indolence became almost proverbial, and it is the subject of some lines in the poem called *A Session of the Poets* ascribed to Rochester. In this poem Apollo passes in review the claims of various poets to the laureateship. He starts with Dryden, but rejects him on account of the rumour that he is going to become a priest. Etherege's turn comes next:

This Reverend Author was no sooner set by,
But *Appollo* had got gentle *George* in his Eye,
And frankly confest, of all Men that writ,
There's none had more fancy, sense, Judgment, and *Wit*;
But i' th' crying Sin, idleness, he was so harden'd,
That his long Seavn' years silence was not to be pardon'd.

As this poem was probably written after the production of
Etherege's third play, Apollo might have had the grace to
admit that Gentle George's seven years' silence had been
amply redeemed. On 11 March 1676, *The Man of Mode or
Sir Fopling Flutter*, a comedy by George Etherege, was produced with great splendour at the Duke's Theatre. The king
was present and the cast was worthy of the occasion; Betterton
played Dorimant, Harris Medley, and Smith Sir Fopling.
The actresses included Mrs Barry, Mrs Betterton and Mrs
Leigh. Dryden contributed a sparkling epilogue, and the
duchess of York allowed the play to be dedicated to her.

The Man of Mode, like its two predecessors, is a picture of
the 'Town' as Etherege knew it, 'a talking play' in Rochester's
words, in which plot is subordinated to the vivid and polished
presentation of certain aspects of contemporary life. Captain
Alexander Radcliffe summed up this new ideal in comedy
when he described Etherege as

> one that does presume to say
> A Plot's too gross for any play:
> Comedy should be clean and neat,
> As Gentlemen do talk and eat.
> So what he writes is but Translation,
> Of Dog and Pa[r]tridge conversation.

Dorimant, the hero of *The Man of Mode*, is the finished
picture of which Sir Frederick Frollick and Courtal and
Freeman are preliminary sketches, the brilliant young aristocrat entirely emancipated from the rules of conventional

morality and leading the life of pleasure with the grace and style of a great artist. Like Oscar Wilde two centuries later, Etherege was a wit and artist in prose who had been admitted to aristocratic circles and was enchanted by the ideal of the fine gentleman who was master of the art of living. Dorimant can be compared to Wilde's Lord Henry Wotton in *The Picture of Dorian Gray*, Lord Darlington in *Lady Winder-mere's Fan* and Viscount Goring in *An Ideal Husband*. The character is based on that of Rochester. Dennis wrote that Dorimant 'had in him several of the Qualities of *Wilmot* Earl of *Rochester*, as, his Wit, his Spirit, his amorous Temper, the Charms he had for the fair Sex, his Falshood and his In-constancy; the agreeable Manner of his chiding his Servants and lastly his repeating, on every occasion, the Verses of Waller'.

The mainspring of the play is the contrast between Dori-mant, the perfect man of wit and fashion, and Sir Fopling Flutter, the coxcomb who has recently 'arriv'd piping hot from Paris' and 'thinks himself the Pattern of Modern Gallantry'. There is probably a good deal of truth in the statement of Dean Lockier that Etherege was 'exactly his own Sir Fopling Flutter'. Indeed he himself wrote in one of his letters from Ratisbon: 'I must confess I am a fop in my heart; ill-customs influence my very senses, and I have been so used to affection that without the help of the air of the Court what is natural cannot touch me'. Sir Fopling is treated lovingly by his creator. Dress and scandal, 'equip-ages' and songs and dancing, which for men like Dorimant and Medley were enjoyed as parts of life which was a work of art are for Sir Fopling simply a means of flattering his own self-importance. The famous passage in which he displays the beauty of his suit, his shoes, his periwig and his gloves (all from famous Parisian shops) to the ladies is the exquisite comedy of a man transformed into a fashion-plate.

In the June following the production of *The Man of Mode* Etherege, with Rochester and some others, took part in a riotous skirmish with the watch at Epsom. It was one of the numerous affairs of the kind which often led to tragic results in the seventeenth century, when gentlemen who drank heavily wore swords. One of the revellers, a Mr Downs, was killed, and a constable was severely injured. Etherege at one point in the proceedings, at any rate, seems to have acted the part of a peacemaker and made 'a submissive oration' to the indignant constable. In December 1677, we hear of him again in trouble, 'squabbling' this time in a tavern with a person called Buckly. Sir Fleetwood Shepherd tried to part the combatants, and, for his pains, was 'runn with a sword under the eye'.

The difficulty of living the life of a Restoration gentleman on a limited income seems to have driven Gentle George at last to adopt the desperate expedient of his own Sir Frederick Frollick. In 1679 he was knighted, and in the same year married 'a rich old widow' called Mary Arnold. The knighthood and the marriage are connected in contemporary reports; it appears that the widow refused to take the dramatist without a title. These things could be bought for hard cash under Charles II, and Etherege probably thought it worth his while to invest some of his capital in purchasing a knighthood in order to obtain control of the widow's fortune. Lady Mary Etherege was a shrew if we can believe contemporary lampoons, several of which contain references to Sir George's conjugal misfortunes:

> Ev'n *gentle George*, with flux in *Tongue* and *Purse*,
> In shunning *one snare* run into a *worse*.
> *Want* once may be relieved in a Mans Life,
> But who can be reliev'd that has a Wife?

It must have been soon after his marriage that he was injured in the collapse of the tennis court at Clare Market.[1] He is said to have been 'dangerously hurt', and perhaps the illness that followed the accident compelled him for once to settle down for a while to lead a quiet life.

For six years Sir George endured the penance of matrimony, but in the spring of 1685 a way of escape presented itself to the unfortunate dramatist. Edmund Poley, the British envoy to the Diet of the Holy Roman Empire at Ratisbon (Regensburg) in Bavaria, was transferred to another post and Sir George Etherege was appointed to succeed him. He 'took leave of his Majesty' (James II) on 30 August, and shortly afterwards left England for the last time, travelling to Ratisbon by way of The Hague.

The Ratisbon mission may be regarded as the last act of the comedy of Gentle George's life, for what followed was merely an epilogue. By one of the chances of history more is known about this act than about any other part of the play. A letter-book containing copies of his correspondence kept by his secretary, Hugh Hughes, has survived[2] and its contents give a vivid picture of the envoy's life at Ratisbon from the autumn of 1685 until his departure in the spring of 1689. Hugh Hughes was a puritanical, priggish, sanctimonious person who had been engaged by Etherege as his secretary before he left England. The choice was a bad one, because of a fundamental incompatibility of temper between the two men, and this was aggravated by a dispute about Hughes's salary. He kept copies of everything in Etherege's correspondence which he thought likely to damage his position, and he sent home long letters full of scandalous gossip about his employer's life and habits.

Sir George seems to have carried out his diplomatic duties efficiently. His despatches are well informed, and, as we

---

[1] See p. 39 above.
[2] Now British Museum Add. MS. 11513.

should expect, contain much shrewd observation of men and manners. He was perfectly well aware of the fact that the men to whom he was writing were courtiers as well as politicians and wanted amusing anecdotes as well as accounts of negotiations, treaties and battles. He was disgusted by the humourless pedantry of the German court which was embodied in the person of the Count de Windisgratz, the Imperial Envoy, a pompous Austrian nobleman, who was a great stickler for etiquette and an absurdly jealous husband. The following character sketch of the Count from a letter addressed by Sir George to Lord Sunderland (dated 9/19 Sept. 1686) is a good example of Etherege's epistolary style; its wit and comic gusto are worthy of the author of *The Man of Mode*:

'The Count de Windisgratz is about 56 years of age, tormented often with the gout, and gravel, which adds to his natural ill humor; he has children by a former wife, which he neglects being fond of some he has by a Lady to whom he has been married some few years. She was [maid] of honor to the Empress Dowager, and esteem'd a great ornament to that Court. She is very like, and full as handsom as, Mrs. Betty Mackerell, but more affected than Mrs. Middleton. The Count is of a temper soe jealous, that he tormented her before her time, when he was her Lover: if he observed her speaking to any man in the Drawing Room he would get her into a Corner, and pinch her black and blew; and she was resolv'd not to have him had not his tears to the Emperess soften'd her to impose her Commands to marry him. He is hott and imperious, and uses those of the Dyet who have some dependance on him as scurvily as he does his Domesticks. He has had experience in affaires, and understands his Master's Interest but will sacrifice anything to his Pride, and ambition; and indeed all his passions are soe violent that he does him little service for want of Conduct. These qualities (some of his Countreymen say) got him this Employment; the ministers at Vienna for their own quiet favouring him in this honourable occasion of his absence. He has been formerly employ'd in the French court, and has twenty times told me, how he was received there; with as much heat, as an old lady tells some pleasant passage of her youth, which warms her. His conversation is soe loud, he is vehement even in trifles, and he speaks french as well as my Lord Peterborough. If you flatter him the Lyon becomes a Lamb, and without examining any thing you advance, will, like the Lord Chamberlain in *Hamlet*, cry "oh very like a Weesel".'[1]

If the English envoy was amazed at the stiffness and formality of the Germans, the inhabitants of Ratisbon were equally surprised at the manners of the English envoy. Etherege seems to have had a typically British contempt for his environment and he led exactly the same sort of life in Bavaria as that to which he had been accustomed at St James's and Covent Garden, 'coaching, fiddling, piping and dancing till two, three or four o'clock in the morning'. According to Hughes, 'the whole town complained of the noise and stir' he and his friends 'made night after night'. At first he found life terribly boring. The Bavarians, he wrote, were 'insensibles à tout hormis la tonnerre'. He sighed for 'the kind nymphs of gentle Thames' and could only console himself with 'a plain Bavarian' with 'sandy locks, brawny limbs and a brick complexion'.

Then a company of players arrived from Nuremberg and among them was a very pretty actress; 'as handsome at least as the Fair Maid of the West which you have seen at New-

---

[1] *The Letter Book of Sir George Etherege*, B.M. Add. MS. 11513, f. 27 v. In the second sentence of the extract the MS. reads 'made', obviously a mistake for 'maid'

market', he writes to Lord Middleton. Even the dour secretary had to admit that this lady 'seemed to have something of grace in her face though none in her manners' Etherege was delighted to find a woman who had something of the wit and charm of the London actresses, and he compares her with Mrs Johnson and Mrs Barry. His connection with her caused a tremendous scandal in Ratisbon, where players were regarded by the German aristocrats as dirt beneath their feet. Gentle George seems to have thoroughly enjoyed shocking the snobs of the imperial city, and he deliberately treated a travelling actress with the courtesy and respect which an English gentleman would have shown to Mrs Betterton or Mrs Barry. He put her 'into his coach before all the company, notwithstanding all the giggling and hissing of the Austrian ladies and of the ministers' wives and daughters, himself humbly walking home on foot'. He even pawned his watch to buy her clothes.

One autumn evening in 1686, when Sir George was dining with his theatrical friend, a company of young louts led by a certain Baron de Sensheim entered his garden and surrounded the house, calling on him to deliver the lady into their hands. They proceeded to whet their swords on the stone walls and pavement. Etherege asked for an hour to consider the proposal, and used the time to arm his servants. He then sallied forth suddenly and inflicted severe punishment on the invaders, though he failed to dislodge them from their positions. Later, he escorted the lady home with an armed guard and the Baron de Sensheim and his followers had to content themselves with 'hooting and hollowing' and shouting 'Great is the Diana of the English Envoy'.

Besides flirtation, Sir George's amusements at Ratisbon included the fashionable card games of basset and ombre, the latest music from London and Paris, coursing, sleighing and tennis. His keen interest in theatrical and literary matters is shown in letters to Betterton, the actor, and Dryden, the poet. The letter to Betterton gives a pleasant picture of musical evenings at the envoy's house: 'I have three in my little family, who now and then give me a little musick; they play very well and at sight. We have all the Operas, and I have a Correspondent at Paris, who sends me what is new there.' Nothing pleased him more than news of his literary friends in London. The success of Sedley's *Bellamira* in May, 1687, recalls the brilliance of Sir Charles's conversation: 'Few of our plays', he writes, 'can boast of more wit than I have heard him speak at a supper.' When a copy of *Bellamira* reaches him it gives him 'that intire Satisfaction', that he 'cannot read it over too often'. When he reads *The Hind and the Panther* he writes with appreciation of Dryden's 'noble ambition to restore poetry to its ancient dignity by wrapping up the mysteries of religion in verse'; but he makes the shrewd comment that 'General Dryden is an Expert Captain, but I allways thought him fitter for execution than for Counsill'. He has a good word too for the young wits Prior and Montague (though he does not know their names) who parodied Dryden's poem.

His thoughts often dwell lovingly on the golden days of the Restoration Carnival. He reminds Dorset of the occasion when he and Etherege 'carried the two dragled tayl'd nymphs one bitter frosty night over the Thames to Lambeth'. He longs for the life of London, with its coffee-houses, its theatres and its good company: 'There is not a day', he writes to his friend Corbet, 'but my thoughts dog you from the Coffee-house to the play, from thence to Marribone. . . . Some of the ancients have imagin'd that the greatest torment of the dead was an impatient longing after what they delighted most in while they were living, and I can swear by my damnation in Germany, this hell is no jesting matter.' 'Remember me', he asks Will Richards, 'to all my friends at the Rose, and do not forget the lilly at the Bar.' But, alas, times were changing and the members of the 'merry gang' were growing staid and respectable. 'Sir Ch: Sidlie setts up for good houres and sobriety; and my Ld Dorset has given over variety, and shuts himself up within my Lady's arms.' Etherege alone remained true to the Epicurean principles of his youth: 'let us still preserve the good humor and our good nature, to make us wellcome near those young people, who possess that plentifull Estat we have pretty well run out of, that we may help them rail at the morose, and cry out with Fallstaff *down with them, they hate us Youth.*'

Etherege's diplomatic career ended in a blaze of glory. He was a loyal supporter of James II, and on 6 July 1688, when he received the news of the birth of an heir to the throne (afterwards the Old Pretender), his joy knew no bounds. He promptly made arrangements for celebrations 'answerable to his Majesty's greatness and the honour of the nation'. His friend Placidus Fleming, Abbot of the Monastery of Scottish Benedictines at Ratisbon, at Sir George's request, was charged with the duty of opening the proceedings with a solemn Te Deum at St James's Church, to which the Imperial Commission and members of the Diplomatic Corps were invited. While the High Mass and Te Deum were being sung '80 pieces of Canon' (obligingly lent by the magistrates of the town) were 'shott off'. In front of the envoy's house two 'large substantiall buildings' were erected. One was a kitchen in which an ox was roasted whole, and the other 'a triumphall piramide' with 'an arbor...in which a consort of Hautbois play'd' and a 'rock out of which three fountaines of wine sprung'. That evening there was a grand dinner at Sir George's house to which all the ministers were invited. They were regaled with no fewer than fifty-two dishes 'loaded with venison and all manner of Fowl' as well as a banquet of sweetmeats and fruit. The sides of the kitchen were removed and the roasted ox given over to the common folk. On the second day the envoy entertained 'all the Ladies and Cavaliers of the neighbourhood' and four hundred pieces of silver were flung to the crowd from the windows. While they were scrambling for the money footmen placed in the windows flung a '3 or 400 hundred squibs to part them who were most mutinous'. 'This', Sir George adds in his account of the affair, 'had an admirable effect, and caused much laughter.' On the third day the guests were the chief magistrates of the city, and Sir George gave them such a feast 'that they own'd they never saw the like'. The culmination of the evening was a carouse for which a great barrel of wine was brought from the English envoy's cellar, and the people were 'told to drink to their Majesties, and the Prince's health'. At the same time, Etherege called for 'three of the biggest glasses' and 'drank them to the chief Magistrate', while 'thirty pieces of Canon were shot off'. Soon after this gargantuan feast news of a very different kind from the joyous tidings of the birth of the Prince of Wales must have reached Sir George. William of Orange landed at Torbay on 5 November and on 3 December James II embarked for France. In February 1689, the vacant throne was offered to William and Mary. Etherege's one principle in politics was unswerving devotion to his master, and he remained loyal to James to the end. As late as 28 January, in a letter to Lord Preston, he refers scornfully to a paper read to the Diet by the Elector of Bavaria, of which the author 'already places the Prince of Orange on the throne, regulating the affairs of England'. When the Revolution was an accomplished fact, it was obvious that Sir George could no longer remain at his post. He seems to have left in haste for Paris, probably in February 1689. Hugh Hughes remained to triumph at Ratisbon, and he vented his spleen against his former master in a vituperative Latin letter addressed to the

treasurers and other senators of Ratisbon. On his departure
from Ratisbon, Sir George left some of his books with his
friend Abbot Fleming, who placed them in the library of his
monastery. They included the works of Shakespeare,
Cowley, Molière, Voiture and Sarasin, and French translations of the *Decameron* of Boccaccio and of some of the
chief Latin poets. Etherege did not survive the Revolution
for long. He appears to have died in Paris 'on or about
10 May 1692', and is said to have been received into the
Roman Catholic Church before his death.

A comparison between Etherege and Oscar Wilde has
already been suggested. Etherege called himself a fop and
Wilde called himself a poseur. Both were, in fact, most truly
themselves when they were acting a part. Like Wilde, too,
Etherege was a poet who expressed himself most successfully
in prose and whose wit was a kind of poetry; and, like Wilde,
he did his best work in prose comedy. Etherege's verse, however, is better than Wilde's because it is less pretentious.
As a writer of verse he has three manners. One is the manner
of popular poetry, the tavern song and the street ballad.
Etherege is the best bacchanalian poet among the wits. The
snatches of drinking song placed in the mouths of Palmer in
The Comical Revenge and Sir Joslin Jolly in *She wou'd if she
cou'd* have an irresistible gaiety, a joyous, dancing rhythm
which keeps them fresh after three centuries. Gatty's song
in *She wou'd if she cou'd* is a little masterpiece in the metre
and style of the street ballad, which anticipates the best work
of Prior and Gay. The second manner is that of the courtly
lyric, the manner of Voiture, Sarasin and Madame de la
Suze. Etherege can play the pastoral game prettily enough,
but he never achieves the felicity of Sedley's best verses in
this style, and, unlike Sedley and Rochester, he can never
transmute the courtly convention into the 'language of the

heart'. His third manner is conversational; it is seen in his two epistles to Lord Middleton from Ratisbon which are simply his witty, graceful conversation put into easily flowing octosyllabic couplets. It is a pity that more of his work in this manner has not survived.

Dryden gave characteristically generous praise to Etherege's prose: 'I will never enter the lists in prose with the undoubted best author of it which our nation has produced.' This is, of course, the hyperbole of friendship, but Gentle George is unquestionably the best prose writer among the Restoration wits. His style is seen at its best in comic dialogue and can be fully appreciated only in its context. Here he is the predecessor and almost certainly the model of Congreve.

Poems by Sir George Etherege

When *Phillis* watch'd her harmless Sheep
　Not one poor Lamb was made a prey;
Yet she had cause enough to weep,
　Her silly heart did go astray:
Then flying to the neighbouring Grove,
She left the tender Flock to rove,
And to the Winds did breathe her Love.
　　She sought in vain
　　To ease her pain;
The heedless winds did fan her fire;
　　Venting her grief
　　Gave no relief;
But rather did encrease desire.
Then sitting with her arms across,
　Her sorrows streaming from each eye;
She fix'd her thoughts upon her loss,
　And in despair resolv'd to die.

From *The Comical Revenge*, 1664, Act II, sc. ii

SONG

Ladies, though to your Conqu'ring eyes
Love owes his chiefest Victories,
And borrows those bright Arms from you
With which he does the world subdue;
  Yet you yourselves are not above
  The Empire nor the Griefs of Love.

Then wrack not Lovers with disdain,
Lest Love on you revenge their Pain;
You are not free because y'are fair;
The Boy did not his Mother spare.
  Beauty's but an offensive dart;
  It is no Armour for the heart.

From *The Comical Revenge,* 1664, Act v, sc. iii

SONG

If she be not kind as fair,
  But peevish and unhandy,
Leave her, she's only worth the care
  Of some spruce Jack-a-dandy.
I wou'd not have thee such an Asse,
  Had'st thou ne're so much leisure,
To sigh and whine for such a Lass
  Whose Pride's above her Pleasure.

Ibid Act ii, sc. iii

GATTY'S SONG

To little or no purpose I spend many days,
In ranging the Park, th' Exchange, and th' Plays;
For ne're in my rambles till now did I prove
So luckie to meet with the man I cou'd love.
Oh! how I am pleas'd when I think on this man,
That I find I must love, let me do what I can!

How long I shall love him, I can no more tell,
Than had I a Fever, when I shou'd be well.
My passion shall kill me before I will show it,
And yet I wou'd give all the world he did know it;
But oh how I sigh, when I think shou'd he woo me,
I cannot deny what I know wou'd undo me!

From *She wou'd if she cou'd*, 1668, Act v, sc. i

CATCH

This is sly and pretty,
And this is wild and witty:
    If either stay'd
    Till she dy'd a Maid,
I' faith 'twould be great pity.

Ibid Act ii, sc. ii

SIR JOSLIN'S SONG

I gave my Love a Green-gown
I' th' merry month of May,
And down she fell as wantonly,
As a Tumbler doth a Play.

From *She wou'd if she cou'd*, 1668, Act v, sc. i

SONG

When first *Amintas* charm'd my heart,
    My heedless Sheep began to stray:
The Wolves soon stole the greatest part,
    And all will now be made a prey.

Ah, let not love your thoughts possess,
'Tis fatal to a Shepherdess;
The dangerous passion you must shun,
Or else like me be quite undone.

From *The Man of Mode*, 1676, Act ii, sc. i

DRINKING SONG

The pleasures of love and the Joyes of good Wine,
To perfect our happiness wisely we joyn.
We to Beauty all day
Give the Soveraign sway,
And her favourite Nymphs devoutly obey.
At the Plays we are constantly making our Court,
And when they are ended we follow the sport
To the Mall and the Park,
Where we love till 'tis dark;
Then sparkling Champaigne
Puts an end to their reign;
It quickly recovers
Poor languishing Lovers,
Makes us frolick and gay, and drowns all our Sorrow.
But alas! we relapse again on the Morrow.
    Let every man stand
    With his glass in his hand,
And briskly discharge at the word of Command.
    Here's a health to all those
    Whom to night we depose:
Wine and beauty in turns great souls should inspire.
Present all together; and now boyes give fire—

Ibid Act IV, sc. i

TO A VERY YOUNG LADY

Sweetest bud of Beauty, may
No untimely frost decay
Th' early glories, which we trace,
Blooming in thy matchless face;
But kindly opening, like the Rose,
Fresh beauties every day disclose,
Such as by *Nature* are not shewn
In all the blossoms she has blown:
And then, what conquest shall you make,
Who hearts already dayly take?
Scorcht in the Morning with thy beams,
How shall we bear those sad extreams
Which must attend thy threatening eyes
When thou shalt to thy Noon arise?

From *A Collection of Poems written upon
Several Occasions by Several Persons* (1672)

TO A LADY, ASKING HIM HOW LONG
HE WOULD LOVE HER

It is not, *Celia*, in our power
  To say how long our love will last,
It may be we within this hour
  May lose those joys we now do taste:
The Blessed, that immortal be,
From change in love are only free.

Then, since we mortal Lovers are,
  Ask not how long our love will last;
But while it does, let us take care
  Each minute be with pleasure past.
Were it not madness to deny
To live, because w'are sure to die?

Ibid

SILVIA

The Nymph that undoes me, is fair and unkind
No less then a wonder by Nature design'd;
She's the grief of my heart, the joy of my eye,
And the cause of a flame that never can die.

Her mouth from whence wit still obligingly flows
Has the beautiful blush, and smell of the rose;
Love and destiny both attend on her will,
She wounds with a look, with a frown she can kill.

The desperate Lover can hope no redress,
Where beauty and rigour are both in excess;
In *Silvia* they meet, so unhappy am I,
Who sees her must love, and who loves her must die.

From *A Collection of Poems written upon
Several Occasions by Several Persons* (1672)

A SONG

Ye happy Swains, whose Hearts are free
   From Love's Imperial Chain,
Take warning and be taught by me,
   T'avoid th' enchanting Pain.
Fatal the Wolves to trembling Flocks,
   Fierce Winds to Blossoms prove,
To careless Seamen hidden Rocks,
   To Human Quiet Love.

Fly the fair Sex, if Bliss you prize;
   The Snake's beneath the Flow'r:
Who ever gaz'd on beauteous Eyes,
   That tasted Quiet more?
How faithless is the Lover's Joy!
   How constant is their Care!
The Kind with Falshood do destroy,
   The Cruel with Despair.

From *The Works of Sir George Etherege:*
Containing his Plays and Poems (1704)

SONG OF BASSETT*

Let Equipage and Dress despair,
    Since *Basset* is come in;
For nothing can oblige the fair
    Like Mony and Morine.*

Is any Countess in Distress,
    She flies not to the Beau;
'Tis only Cony* can redress
    Her Grief with a *Rouleau*.*

By this bewitching Game betray'd,
    Poor Love is bought and sold;
And that which should be a free Trade
    Is now ingross'd by Gold.

Ev'n Sense is brought into Disgrace
    Where Company is met,
Or silent stands, or leaves the Place,
    While all the Talk's *Basset*.

Why, Ladies, will you stake your Hearts,
    Where a plain Cheat is found?
You first are rook'd out of those Darts
    That gave your selves the Wound.

The Time, which should be kindly lent
    To Plays and witty Men,
In waiting for a Knave is spent,
    Or wishing for a Ten.

Title *Bassett:* an obsolete game of cards, resembling Faro, first played at Venice (*O.E.D.*).

4 *Morine* or moreen: a stout woollen or woollen and cotton material (*O.E.D.*), presumably used for covers of card tables, like baize in later times.

7 *Cony:* a gull.

8 *Rouleau:* a number of gold coins made up into a cylindrical packet (*O.E.D.*).

Stand in defence of your own Charms,
    Throw down this Favourite,
That threatens, with his dazzling Arms,
    Your Beauty and your Wit.

What Pity 'tis, those Conquering Eyes,
    Which all the World subdue,
Shou'd, while the Lover gazing dies,
    Be only on *Alpue*!*

From *The Works of Sir George Etherege* (1704)

32 *Alpue* or Alpieu: in the game of basset, a mark put on a card to indicate
that the player doubles his stake after winning (*O.E.D.*).

THE FORSAKEN MISTRESS

A Dialogue between Phillis and Strephon

PHILLIS Tell me, gentle *Strephon*, why
You from my Embraces fly?
Does my Love thy Love destroy?
Tell me, I will yet be coy.
    Stay, O stay, and I will feign
(Though I break my Heart) Disdain;
But, lest I unkind appear,
For ev'ry Frown I'll shed a Tear.
    And if in vain I court thy Love,
Let mine, at least, thy Pity move:
Ah! while I scorn vouchsafe to woo;
Methinks you may dissemble too.

STREPHON Ah! Phillis, that you would contrive
A way to keep my Love alive;
But all your other Charms must fail,
When Kindness ceases to prevail.
    Alas! no less than you, I grieve,
My dying Flame has no Reprieve;
For I can never hope to find,
Shou'd all the Nymphs I court be kind,
One Beauty able to renew
Those Pleasures I enjoy'd in you,
When Love and Youth did both conspire
To fill our Breasts and Veins with Fire.
    'Tis true some other Nymph may gain
That Heart which merits your Disdain;
But second Love has still Allay,
The Joys grow aged, and decay.
Then blame me not in losing more
Than Love and Beauty can restore;
And let this Truth thy comfort prove,
I wou'd, but can no longer love.

From *The Works of Sir George Etherege* (1704)

TWO EPISTLES TO LORD MIDDLETON
FROM RATISBON

I. *To my Lord Middleton:*
with following Copie of Verses

From hunting Whores, and hanting play,
And minding nothing else all day
And all the night too you will say,
To make grave legs in formal fetters,
Converse with Fops, and write dull Letters,
To goe to bed 'twixt eight and nine,
And sleep away my precious time
In such an idle sneaking place,
Where vice and folly hide their face
And in a troublesome disguise
The wife seems modest, husband wise.
For pleasure here has the same fate
Which does attend affaires of State,
The Plague of Ceremony infects,
Ev'n in Love, the softer Sex;
Who an essential will neglect
Rather than loose the least respect.
With regular approach we Storm,
And never visit but in form,
That is, sending to know before
At what o'Clock they'll play the whore.
The nymphs are constant, Gallants private,
One scarce can guesse who 'tis they drive at.
This seems to me a scurvy fashion,
Who have been bred in a free nation
With Liberty of Speech, and passion.
Yet I cannot forbear to Spark it,
And make the best of a bad market.
Meeting with one, by chance, kind hearted,
Who noe preliminaries started,

I enter'd, beyond expectation,
Into a close negotiation:
Of which hereafter a Relation.
Humble to fortune not her Slave,
I still was pleas'd with what she gave;
And, with a firm, and cheerfull minde,
I steer my cours with every wind,
To all the Ports she has design'd.

This and the poem on the next page are preserved in Etherege's Ratisbon Letter-book. The title and the numbering have been added by the present editor. The first epistle was sent to Lord Middleton on 9/19 January 1685/6 and the second on 19/29 April 1686. Charles, second earl of Middleton (1640–1719), to whom the two epistles were addressed, was secretary of state under James II and was Etherege's official superior. The epistles were both printed with slight variations in collections that appeared in 1696, 1697 and 1704 and also directly from the MS. by Miss S. Rosenberg in her edition of *The Letter-book of Sir George Etherege* (Oxford University Press, 1928). Dryden, apparently at the request of Middleton, wrote *A Letter to Sir George Etherege* in reply to no. II in the same metre and style which will be found in the collected editions of his works (see *The Poetical Works of John Dryden*, ed. G. R. Noyes, pp. 214, 215 and Noyes's note).

II. *The Verses*

Since Love and verse, as well as Wine,
Are brisker where the sun doth shine,
'Tis something to loose two degrees,*
Now age it self begins to freez,
Yet this I patiently cou'd bear
If the Rough Danube's Beauties were
But onely two degrees less faire
Than the Kind Nymphs of gentle Thames
Who warme me hither with their beames.
Such power they have they can dispense
Five hundred Miles their Influence.
But hunger forces men to eat,
Tho' no temptation's in the meat.
How wou'd the ogling Sparks dispise
The Darling Damsel of my eyes,
Did they behold her at a Play
As she's trick'd up on holiday,
When the whole family combine
For publick pride to make her shine.
Her Hair which long befor lay matted
Are in this day comb'd out and pleated,
A Diamond bodkin in each tress
The badges of her nobleness;
For ev'ry Stone, as well as she,
Can boast an ancient Pedegree.
These form'd the Jewell erst did grace
The Cap o' th' first Graff* o' th' Race,
Now preferr'd by Gräffin* Marian

3 *...two degrees:* Etherege's geography is muddled; he seems to have
thought that Ratisbon (Regensburg) was two degrees further north than
London. Actually it is over two degrees further south.

27, 28 *Graff...Gräffin*: German titles equivalent to count and countess.

T'adorne the handle of her fan.
And, as by old record appears,
Worn since in Kunigunda's* ears,
Now sparkling in the Fräuleins hair:
No Serpent* breaking in the Air
Can with her starry head compare.
Such Ropes of Pearls her hands incumber
She Scarce can deal the Cards at Ombre.*
So many Rings each finger fraight
They tremble with the mighty weight;
The like in England nere was seen—
Since Holbin drew Hall* and his Queen.
But after these fantastick sights
The lustre's meaner than the lights;
For she that bears this glitt'ring Pomp
Is but a tawdry ill-bred Rampe*
Whose brawny Limbs and martiall face
Proclaime her of the Gothick Race,
More than the painted pagentrie
Of all her father's Heraldry;
But there's another sort of Creatures,
Whose ruddy Look and grotesq features
Are soe much out of nature's way,
You'd think them stamp'd on other clay:
No lawfull daughters of old Adam—
From these behold a Citty madam
With Arms in mittins, head in muff,
A dapper cloack, and rev'rend ruff:

31 *Kunigunda:* a famous Bavarian duchess of the sixteenth century of whom Etherege would have heard in the Bavarian city of Regensburg. The name is misprinted as 'Renigunda' in the old editions.

33 *Serpent:* a kind of firework.

36 *Ombre:* fashionable seventeenth-century card game.

40 *Hall:* Henry VIII.

44 *Rampe:* 'a bold, vulgar, ill-behaved woman or girl' (*O.E.D.*).

No farce so pleasant as this Maukin,*
The pretty jett she has in walking
And the soft sound of high Dutch talking.

Here unattended by the Graces,
The Queen of Love in a sad Case is,
Nature, her Active Minister,
Neglects affairs and will not stir;
Thinks it not worth her while to please,
But when she does it for her ease.

Evn I, her most Devout Adorer,
With wand'ring thoughts appear before her;
And when I'm making an oblation,
Am fain to Spurr Imagination
With some old London inclination.

The bow is bent at German Dame,
The arrow flys at English Game.

Kindness, that can indifference warm,
And blow that calm into a Storm,
Has in the very tendrest hour
Over my gentleness no pow'r,
True to my Country women's charms
Whilst Kiss'd and press'd in forraigne Arms.

From *The Letter-Book of Sir George Etherege*,
B.M. Add. MS. 11513, ff. 5 v. 6, 15, 16

57 *Maukin:* 'an untidy female…slut, slattern, drab' (*O.E.D.*).

Charles Sackville,
Earl of Dorset

For pointed Satyrs, I wou'd Buckhurst *choose,*
The best good Man, *with the worst natur'd* Muse.
ROCHESTER, *An Allusion to Horace,* ll. 59, 60

Charles Sackville, Earl of Dorset
1638–1706

EDWARD SACKVILLE, fourth earl of Dorset, writing on 5 October 1645, to the countess of Middlesex, mentions his grandson, who was also a grandson of the countess: 'the little hopeful boy, one Mr. Charles Sackville, thatt when you are melancholy, will grow up, to make you merry.' The child mentioned in this letter was not yet three years old. He was the son of Richard Sackville, Lord Buckhurst, the earl of Dorset's eldest son, and his wife, Lady Frances (*née* Cranfield), daughter of the earl and countess of Middlesex. Their marriage had sealed an alliance between the Sackvilles and the Cranfields, two great families of seventeenth-century England, both of middle-class origin. The Sackvilles, of Knole Park in Kent, had achieved wealth and greatness under the Tudors. Sir Richard Sackville, a successful barrister and civil servant, was a cousin of Anne Bullen and under-treasurer of the Exchequer in the reign of Henry VIII. His son, Thomas, one of the most brilliant figures of the Elizabethan age, was distinguished both as a poet and a statesman. He was the author of the famous Induction to *The Mirror for Magistrates* and part-author of *Gorboduc*, the first English tragedy in blank verse; he was also one of Elizabeth's most trusted councillors, and he succeeded Burghley as lord treasurer. The queen granted him the beautiful manor of Knole in Kent and raised him to the peerage as Baron Buckhurst, and James I created him earl of Dorset. His grandson, Edward Sackville, the fourth earl, was celebrated for his beauty, his wealth, his duel with Edward Bruce, and his alleged liaison with Venetia Stanley. He was lord chamberlain to Queen Henrietta Maria and his wife was governess to the children of Charles I.

Lionel Cranfield, first earl of Middlesex, like Sir Richard Sackville a century before, was a wealthy citizen who, through his financial ability and his dextrous alliances with powerful courtiers, made his way into the ranks of the aristocracy. He became lord treasurer in 1621, and through the influence of his wife's cousin, the all-powerful George Villiers, duke of Buckingham, was created earl of Middlesex in 1622. His home, Copt Hill, in Epping Forest, was, like Knole, a house of great beauty and celebrated for its hospitality. By his wife Anne, described as 'a bouncing sort of Lady Mayoress', he had several children, one of whom was the Lady Frances, who married Richard Sackville, Lord Buckhurst. Like most of the Sackvilles, this Lord Buckhurst, who became fifth earl of Dorset on the death of his father in 1652, was interested in literature. He wrote a poem in memory of Ben Jonson and collaborated with his tutor, Joseph Rutter, in a translation of the *Cid* of Corneille, the first English version of a French classical tragedy, published in 1637.

The young Charles Sackville, now Lord Buckhurst, entered Westminster School as a boarder with his brothers Richard and Edward in 1657. He spent only a year there, however, under the headmastership of the formidable Richard Busby. In 1658 he went abroad, travelled in France and Italy with his tutor, John Jennings, and returned to England soon after the Restoration.

Charles II, who never forgot the friends of his youth, showered honours on the son of his former governess, who became one of the leaders of the 'merry gang' at court in the years immediately following the Restoration. He was a stout, good-natured, voluptuous young man with a satiric wit, and, like all his family, was fond of literature and the society of men of letters. As early as August 1662, we hear of plans for a joint translation of *La Mort de Pompée*, a tragedy of Corneille to be executed by the veteran poet Edmund Waller and a group of young courtiers, including Buckhurst and Sedley. This version was acted in October 1663, and Buckhurst seems to have been responsible for the translation of the fourth act.[1]

Soon after the Restoration the young Lord Buckhurst was involved in two serious scrapes. In February, 1661/2 he and his brother Edward and some other young men mistook a tanner called John Hoppy for a highwayman on the road at Stamford Hill, near Tottenham. There was a scuffle and John Hoppy was mortally wounded. The young men were indicted for murder, confessed to manslaughter, and were pardoned by the king. Gossip was busy with the affair and Pepys heard a highly coloured version of it, according to which the young men had committed highway robbery and murder. The second escapade was the notorious rag at Oxford Kate's.[2] At the trial which followed, Sir Robert Foster, the Lord Chief Justice of the King's Bench, 'heard that my Lord Buckhurst was there' and 'asked whether it was that Buckhurst who was lately tried for robbery; and when answered Yes, he asked whether he had so soon forgot his deliverance at that time, and that it would have more become him to have been at his prayers begging God's forgiveness, than now running into such courses again'. Buckhurst was only nineteen at this time, so it was probably in consideration of his youth that no penalty was inflicted upon him. Rochester was doubtless thinking of the killing of Hoppy and the rag at Oxford Kate's when he said 'he did not know how it was, but my Lord Dorset [Buckhurst] might do

[1] See above, p. 34.
[2] See above, p. 29.

anything, yet was never to blame'. Strangely enough, on 16 June 1663, the day on which Sedley and Buckhurst were carousing at Oxford Kate's, there was a tremendous thunderstorm at Wythiam, a village in Sussex which was the original home of the Sackvilles. The parish church, where Buckhurst's ancestors were buried, was destroyed, the bells melted by the lightning and the family monuments 'torn in pieces'.

In October 1664, war broke out with Holland, and Buckhurst, with other young courtiers, went as volunteers to the fleet, serving under the command of the duke of York in his flagship, the *Royal Charles*. In the months following the outbreak of the war the duke's squadron was patrolling the Channel in expectation of an attack by the Dutch admiral Opdam. On 1 December Buckhurst wrote to his uncle, Lionel Cranfield, earl of Middlesex, complaining of the 'tedious voyage' from Portsmouth and anticipating a meeting with the Dutch which might 'empty our ship where at present the crowd is intolerable'. It was probably during those dark, wintry days of December 1664, when Buckhurst was being tossed in the Channel in a crowded seventeenth-century warship that he composed his most sparkling and delightful poem, the famous ballad 'To all you ladies now at land'. We are told that he was very fond of the popular English ballad poetry, and that he made a large collection of broadsides. 'To all you ladies now at land' is a true popular ballad written to the tune of an older ballad called 'Shackerley Hay'. It was published anonymously as a broadside and was entered on the Stationers' Register on 30 December as *The Noble Seaman's Complaint to the Ladies at land*. The price was sixpence, and Pepys, like Buckhurst a lover of ballad poetry, bought a copy as soon as it appeared. On 2 January he went to a party at Lord Brouncker's house and 'occasioned much mirth' by reading the new ballad and ascribing its authorship in jest to three distinguished admirals, Sir George Askew, Sir William Penn and Sir John Lawson. Many years later Prior, in his dedication of his poems to Buckhurst's son, wrote that the song was 'written the night before the engagement with the Dutch in 1665' (i.e. the naval battle off Lowestoft on 3 June 1665), and this story has been commonly repeated, though Dr Johnson doubted its truth. He heard from 'the late Earl of Orrery, who was likely to have good hereditary intelligence, that Lord Buckhurst had been a week employed upon it, and only retouched or finished it on the memorable evening'.[1]

Except for Prior's statement and the vague tradition mentioned by Lord Orrery to Dr Johnson, there is no evidence that Buckhurst was present at the fierce naval engagement fought off Lowestoft on 3 June 1665. It was on this day that Dryden laid the scene of his *Essay of Dramatick Poesie*, in which he describes the meeting of the four friends, Lisideius (Sedley), Crites (Howard), Eugenius (Buckhurst) and Neander (Dryden), and their trip down the river towards the sounds of the gunfire off the East Coast which could be heard in London. The Essay must not, of course, be regarded as a literal record of fact, but it is highly probable that it was based on a real conversation between the four men, though Dryden's memories had certainly passed through the 'deep well' of the creative imagination and had been transmuted into an admirable work of art. In the *Essay* Buckhurst is represented as a stout defender of the moderns against the ancients and of the old English tradition in the drama as against the new-fangled classicism of the French: 'Though I never judged the plays of the Greek or Roman poets comparable to ours, yet, on the other side, those we now see acted come short of many which were written in the last age.' The *Essay* is dedicated to Buckhurst in very complimentary

[1] Johnson, 'Life of Dorset' in *Lives of the Poets*.

terms, and in the Epistle Dedicatory Dryden writes of the speakers that 'they differed in their opinions, as 'tis probable they would neither do I take upon me to reconcile but to relate them...without passion or interest'. He would certainly not have addressed these words to Buckhurst unless the dialogue recorded in the *Essay* had borne a definite relation to actual conversations between the four speakers.

Of the various women with whom the young Lord Buckhurst amused himself in those very merry dancing, drinking, laughing, quaffing years, the most famous is Nell Gwyn, the pretty, vivacious actress who started her theatrical career as an orange girl and then became a very successful performer in comedy and the mistress of the actor Charles Hart, whom she called her Charles I. Buckhurst is said to have first seen her in a farce called *All Mistaken or The Mad Couple*, in which she rolled across the stage with a fat man and displayed a shapely leg which attracted the young nobleman's attention. On 13 July 1667, Pepys heard from his friend Mr Pierce that 'My Lord Buckhurst hath got Nell away from the King's House, lies with her and gives her £100 a year, so as she hath sent her parts to the house, and will act no more'. Two days later the diarist was dining at 'The King's Head' at Epsom and he heard that Buckhurst, Nell and Sedley were lodging next door and 'keeping merry house'. 'Poor girl!' he adds, 'I pity her; but more the loss of her at the King's house.' By 22 August Nell was back at Drury Lane and acting in Dryden's *The Indian Emperour*. On the 26th Orange Moll, the Captain of the Orange Girls at the King's House, told Pepys that 'Nell is already left by my Lord Buckhurst, and that he makes sport of her, and swears she hath had all she could get of him; and Hart her great admirer, now hates her'. This appears to have been the end of Nell's liaison with Buckhurst. Soon after she became the mistress of Charles II (her 'Charles III'). Scandal said that Buckhurst was compensated for the loss of his mistress by various favours which he received from the king. According to a pamphlet called *Flagellum Parliamentarium* ascribed to Andrew Marvell, 'Buckhurst with a good will parted with his play wench, and in gratitude is made one of the Bedchamber; has the ground of the wardrobe given him, and £6,000 at three several times'. It is true that Buckhurst was made first groom and afterwards gentleman of the Bedchamber with an annual salary of one thousand pounds, and was also granted a piece of land on the site of the Great Wardrobe. There is no real reason, however, to suppose that these royal bounties were connected with Nell Gwyn. The Sackvilles were attached to the Stuarts by strong bonds of hereditary friendship. Buckhurst's mother had looked after the king in his youth and he himself had been an intimate friend of Charles since he first appeared at court. He had received signal marks of the royal favour before Nell appeared on the London stage.

Buckhurst, Sedley and Buckingham were close allies in the pursuits of what Dr Johnson calls 'riotous and licentious pleasures' in the year 1668. All three were seen in the pit at the first performance of Etherege's *She wou'd if she cou'd* at the Duke's House in Lincoln's Inn Fields on 6 February. In September they were accompanying the king on a royal progress through East Anglia and, according to Pepys's friend Mr Pierce, 'the king and these gentlemen did make the fiddlers of Thetford...sing them all the bawdy songs they could think of'. At Saxham the king was drunk with 'Sidly, Buckhurst &c.' one night when Lord Arlington arrived, and 'would not give him audience, or could not'. When the duke of York reproached Baptist May for 'occasioning the king's giving himself up to these gentlemen' and 'neglecting my lord Arlington', May answered 'merrily, that, by God, there was no man in England that had heads to lose, durst do what they do, every day, with the King'. That autumn Buckhurst was

racketing about London with Sedley and, if Pepys's infor-
mant is to be believed, on one occasion they ran 'up and down
all night with their arses bare, through the streets; and at last
fighting, and being beat by the watch' were 'clapped up all
night' by a constable who was 'chid and imprisoned for his
pains'.

The graceless scamp of these escapades was, however, like
his friend Sedley, a man of taste and a good judge of literature. One day in 1669 he was 'beating about for books to his
taste' in Little Britain, the booksellers' quarter. When he was
looking round a certain shop, probably that of T. Helder, at
the Sign of the Angel, he picked up by chance a volume containing a long poem in blank verse. He read a few lines and
was so struck by them that he bought it 'for a trifle'. The
poem was *Paradise Lost*. Buckhurst took it home, 'read it
many times over' and sent it to Dryden to get his opinion
of it. Dryden had never seen the poem before; but his verdict
was instant and decisive: 'That poet had cutt us all out.' If
this story is true there is irony in the indebtedness of Milton
to one of the 'sons of Belial' for introducing the great
Puritan epic to the literary public.

In the years 1669 and 1670 Buckhurst visited the court of
Louis XIV three times in an official capacity. He was presented to the French king in the summer of 1669 and received
from him one of his portraits set in diamonds. In May, 1670,
when Henriette d'Orléans, the sister of Charles II, came to
Dover to negotiate a secret treaty with her brother, Buckhurst was sent immediately to Dunkirk to beg from Louis
permission for her to remain ten days longer on English soil,
and, finally, in July 1670, he accompanied Buckingham to
France with the special mission to return the compliment
which Louis had paid to Charles by sending the Maréchal
de Bellefonds to condole with him on the death of Henriette.
This mission included a galaxy of the wits, Buckingham,

Buckhurst, Sedley, Sprat, Samuel Butler (author of *Hudibras*) and Joe Haines, the comic actor. They were magnificently entertained by Louis at Versailles with feasting, music, a mock naval battle on the canal and the performance of a pastoral play.

Lionel Cranfield, third earl of Middlesex, Buckhurst's maternal uncle, died on 27 October 1674. Buckhurst inherited his large estates worth three thousand pounds per annum, and a royal warrant was issued on 20 January 1675, to grant him the titles of Baron Cranfield and earl of Middlesex. For some time before these events, Buckhurst's name had been coupled with that of the widow of the earl of Falmouth, who had been killed in the naval battle off Lowestoft in 1665. Mary, countess of Falmouth, a maid of honour of the duchess of York, was twenty-nine in 1674 and was the daughter of a Warwickshire gentleman, Colonel Hervey Bagot. Pepys, who saw her in June, 1666, calls her 'a pretty woman...now in her second or third mourning, and pretty pleasant in her looks'. Anthony Hamilton gives a vivid word-picture of her: 'she had beautiful and regular features, and that sort of brown complexion, which, when in perfection, is so particularly fascinating, and more especially in England, where it is uncommon. There was an involuntary blush almost continually on her cheek....' The countess had a bad reputation, and gossip said she had been a mistress of the king. Buckhurst's parents were alarmed by the reports that she was married to their son. The date of the marriage is uncertain, but the new earl of Middlesex acknowledged it as soon as the death of his uncle gave him an independent estate. Whatever truth there may be in the gossip about Lady Falmouth, there is no doubt that her second marriage was a love match. Some extant letters[1] from Buckhurst are written

[1] One of these letters has the superscription 'For the Countess of Falmouth'. The others are almost certainly addressed to the same person.

in a vein of passionate sincerity which convinces the reader
that he is not merely paying a courtly compliment when he
declares to the Countess: 'You alone have government not
only of my actions, but of my very thoughts.'

On 27 August 1677, the fifth earl of Dorset died. Unlike
most members of his family, he was dull, morose and un-
generous. On his death his son succeeded to his title and to
his large estates. Charles Sackville was now earl of Dorset and
Middlesex, and at the age of thirty-five was master of the
wealth accumulated by two of the most successful of the
acquisitive families who had carved out fortunes for themselves in the economic revolution which began with the dis-
solution of the monasteries. His married life with Lady
Falmouth seems to have been happy, but it did not last for
long. The new countess died in childbed in 1679, but death
did not deliver her from the coarse gibes of contemporary
lampooners. In the November following her death Mulgrave's scurrilous *Essay on Satyr* was being circulated in
manuscript. The character sketch of Dorset is the wittiest
passage in this poem. It contains malicious insinuations concerning the dead countess, but there is probably a good deal
of truth in the description of the earl as degenerating at this
time into a besotted idler:

> Thus *D—t* purring like a thoughtful Cat,
> Married, but wiser, puss [ne'er] thought of that:
> And first he worried her with railing rhime,
> Like *Pembrook's* Mastives at his kindest time;
> Then for one night sold all his slavish Life,
> A teeming Widow but a barren Wife;
> Suckl'd by contract of such a fulsome toad,
> He lugg'd about the matrimonial load;
> Till fortune blindly kind as well as she,
> Has ill restor'd him to his liberty;

Which he would use in all his sneaking way,
Drinking all night, and dosing all the day;
Dull as *Ned Howard*, whom his brisker Times,
Had fam'd for dulness in malicious Rhimes;...[1]

Mulgrave's sketch of Dorset is corroborated by a passage in a letter written by Nell Gwyn in her strange orthography to Lawrence Hyde, probably in June 1678: 'My lord of Dorset apiers wouse [i.e. appears once] in thre munthe, for he drinkes aile with Shadwell and Mr Haris at the Dukes House all day long.'

Dorset was one of the peers who assembled at Oxford when the king summoned Parliament to meet there in March 1681. The years of riotous living had made inroads on his constitution and he fell down in a fit of apoplexy in the King's bedchamber. To recuperate from the illness which followed this attack, he went to France and visited Henry Savile, the English ambassador in Paris. According to the charitable gossip of the time, they enjoyed themselves 'talking blasphemy and atheisme, drinking, and perhaps that which is worse'. It was also reported that he was courting Madame la Gouvernette, a wealthy young Huguenot lady. This rumour seems to have been without foundation, but Dorset was constantly being pestered by his mother with requests that he should marry again. The dowager was anxious about the wild life which he continued to lead, and her letters to him show that she hoped marriage would have a sobering effect: 'I doe passionately long to see you fixt.' Finally he gave way, and in June 1685, married Lady Mary Compton, a beautiful girl of twenty-three, daughter of the earl of Northampton. She brought him a jointure of fourteen thousand pounds.

---

[1] *The Fourth (and last) Collection of Poems, Satyrs, Songs, &c.* (London, 1689), pp. 30, 31. The text of l. 2 of this extract is obviously corrupt. In place of 'near', which is certainly a misprint, I have read 'ne'er', and have inserted a comma after 'Married'.

Dorset walked in the train of Mary of Modena at the coronation of James II and carried the queen's ivory sceptre. Immediately after his accession to the throne, James paid the arrears of his salary as gentleman of the bedchamber and confirmed him in his lord lieutenancy of Sussex. Soon, however, Dorset, who was no friend to the new king's religious views, retired from the court and spent most of his time at Copt Hall with his young wife, who bore him a son, Lionel Cranfield Sackville, on 18 June 1686/7. 'My Ld Dorset', wrote Etherege from Ratisbon, 'has given over variety, and shuts himself up within my Lady's arms', and in a bantering passage in one of his letters he tells Lord Middleton that he 'may be grown as temperate as Sir Charles Sedley and as uxorious as my lord Dorset'. The second Lady Dorset may not have been such a dazzling figure as her predecessor, but she seems to have had a sobering effect on the earl, who, like his friend Sedley, was now settling down at last to a quiet life after the years of racketing about Whitehall and Covent Garden. Early in the new reign it had been rumoured that Dorset was to lose his lord lieutenancy. Actually it was not until January 1687/8 that he gave up his commission. The king had ordered the lords lieutenant to issue a questionnaire to their deputies and justices of the peace asking them how they would act at a general election. Dorset, with many other noblemen, refused to have anything to do with this unconstitutional procedure. His commission as lord lieutenant of Sussex was promptly taken from him and given to Lord Montague of Cowdray. He was one of the twenty-one temporal peers who offered to go bail for the seven bishops sent to the Tower by King James in June 1688, and he also appeared at Westminster Hall with many other peers to support the bishops at their trial. Throughout the sequence of events which led up to the Revolution, he seems to have acted under the guidance of Henry Compton, bishop of London, his wife's uncle. He did not sign the invitation to the prince of Orange to come to England in the autumn of 1688, but after the prince had landed at Torbay he helped the Princess Anne to escape from Whitehall, and, together with the bishop of London, escorted her to Nottingham. After James had fled to France, Dorset was one of the council of peers which sat daily in London to conduct public business, and at the Convention Parliament in February 1688/9, he voted in favour of the resolutions declaring the throne vacant and offering it to William and Mary. The day after the accession of the new sovereigns Dorset was appointed Lord Chamberlain of the King's Household.

One of his earliest and most unpleasant duties as Lord Chamberlain was to deprive his old friend John Dryden of the offices of Poet Laureate and Historiographer Royal, because he refused to take the oaths of allegiance to William and Mary. However, to compensate the poet for the financial loss, Dorset out of his own purse made him what Dryden himself calls 'a most bountiful present'. This is one of the many examples of the generosity to men of letters for which he was celebrated. Almost every professional writer of any note and many of the smaller fry of Grub Street profited in one way or another by Dorset's open-handed bounty. Dryden, Shadwell, Crowne, Etherege, Nahum Tate, D'Urfey, Prior, Tom Brown and many others enjoyed the lavish hospitality of Knole and Copt Hall, and some of them received welcome financial aid from the master of those famous houses. Dorset's encouragement to men of letters was not confined to invitations to Knole and presents of guineas. He visited Oldham, when that poet was a poor usher in a school at Croydon; he is said to have introduced Butler's *Hudibras* to the court of Charles II; and, by means of his praise, he ensured the success of Wycherley's *The Plain Dealer*, which, at first, was badly received by the public. He took the young Matthew Prior from his uncle's tavern, and paid for his education at Westminster and Cambridge. Shadwell, who succeeded Dryden as Laureate, was treated as one of the family at Copt Hall, and there he wrote part of one of his best comedies, *The Squire of Alsatia*. Dorset and Sedley are said to have helped him by writing whole scenes for his plays. In an epistle which is a masterpiece of courtly compliment the young William Congreve dedicated his third comedy, *Love for Love*, to the Lord Chamberlain, who had read and approved it in manuscript. On the whole, Macaulay's glowing panegyric of Dorset as a patron of literature seems justified: 'Such a patron of letters England had never seen. His bounty was bestowed with equal judgment and liberality, and was confined to no sect or faction. Men of genius estranged from each other by literary jealousy or by difference of political opinion, joined in acknowledging his impartial kindness.'

Dorset might, no doubt, have played a prominent part in politics after the Revolution, but he contented himself with carrying out his duties as Lord Chamberlain, which included the congenial, though not always easy, task of supervising the two licensed theatrical companies. He was also one of the Lord Justices or Regents who were appointed to assist Queen Mary during the absence of her husband on the Continent. In spite of malicious reports that he flirted with the Jacobites, he seems to have served King William faithfully, and on one occasion he spent a cold January night with the king tossing in an open boat on the breakers off the Dutch coast. He was one of the founders, and, perhaps, the first president of the most famous of Whig clubs, the Kit-Cat, and two of his married daughters were among the beauties whose names were inscribed on the club's celebrated collection of toasting glasses.

Dorset resigned his office of Lord Chamberlain in 1697. His second wife had died in 1691. In October 1704, he married a woman called Anne Roche whom he had probably employed as a housekeeper, and in the last two years of his life he sank into a miserable dotage. His third wife is said to have 'suffered few persons to approach him during his last illness, or rather decay, and was supposed to have converted his weakness of mind to her own objects of acquisition'. He grew fat and apoplectic and suffered from the spleen. In these last years, according to Swift he was a 'very dull companion'. He was taken ill at Bath in January 1705/6, and died there on the 26th. A flash of gaiety of the old companion of Sedley and Rochester returned to him on his deathbed. William Congreve, who visited him at Bath, reported that he 'slab-bered more wit when he was dying than most men when they are in good health'.

Dorset was the least productive of all the Restoration wits. His works consist of the translation of Act IV of *La Mort de Pompée*, a few short satires, prologues and epilogues in the couplet, the famous ballad 'To all you ladies now at land', and a handful of lyrics, the most notable of which are certainly the sequence inspired by Katherine Sedley. In 1668 Dryden had expressed the hope that his dedication of the *Essay of Dramatick Poesie* might awaken in Lord Buckhurst (as he was then) the 'desire of writing something in whatever kind it be, which might be an honour to our age and country'. The young nobleman was, however, probably too rich and too indolent to undertake a work on a large scale. The condition of a wealthy and universally flattered patron, 'fed with soft dedications all day long', is, perhaps, even worse for the creative artist than poverty and obscurity. Dorset's little sheaf of poems were, however, greatly admired by the men of the Augustan age. When Dryden couples his name with those of Shakespeare, Virgil and Donne, and Prior declares that 'There is a Lustre in His Verses, like That of the Sun in Claude Loraine's Landskips; it looks Natural, and is Inimitable', we are, of course, listening to the hyperboles of courtly friendship. Pope, however, who had no personal acquaintance with him and was under no obligation to the Sackvilles, certainly had a very high opinion of Dorset's poetry, and studied it carefully. In conversation with Joseph Spence he is reported to have said: 'Lord Dorset is the best of all those writers.' 'What!' answered Spence in surprise, 'better than Lord Rochester?' 'Yes', was the reply, 'Rochester has neither so much delicacy or exactness as Lord Dorset.' Modern readers will probably share Spence's amazement at this verdict. To them it will seem that Dorset's poems have neither the lyrical beauty of Sedley's best work nor the dynamic power and intellectual distinction of Rochester's. Pope, however, was probably thinking in terms of the development of Augustan satire and was referring chiefly to Dorset's work in the couplet. Certainly in his two little satires on the Honourable Edward Howard, author of the 'incomparable incomprehensible Poem called British Princes', he writes lines which are almost worthy of the author of *The Dunciad* (see pp. 128–131).

As a lyrical poet Dorset is, perhaps, nearer to Etherege than any other member of the 'merry gang'. His masterpiece, 'To all you ladies now at land' (see p. 133), has an effervescent gaiety like that of Gentle George's best songs. Using the form of the street ballad and helped, no doubt, by the popular tune for which he is writing, Dorset here produces a delicious dance of words with a nicely balanced combination of irony, humour, wit and lyrical sweetness. The poem is a sort of caricature of the attitude of the courtly lover, but, like all good caricatures, it is the work of an artist who understands and admires the thing he is mocking. 'We live in an age that's more civil and wise, than to follow the rules of romances.' Dorset exclaims in another poem, yet the 'rules of romances' are not dead as far as Dorset is concerned; they are still loved for their grace and their beauty, though they seem slightly ridiculous in an age grown 'civil and wise'. The frank, hearty, sensual song of 'bonny Black Bess' is another poem in the manner of the broadsides. The tune is the same as that of Gatty's song in *She wou'd if she cou'd*, and, like Etherege's poem, this song grows straight out of the life of the park, the theatre, the street and the court, the coloured, bustling pageant of Restoration London.

Dorset's most original and individual work is to be found in the sequence of four little poems on Katherine Sedley.[1] The character of that remarkable woman seems to have fascinated him, and the four poems, only one of which is dated, seem to be sketches of her at four different stages in her career. Rochester was probably thinking of these poems when he called Dorset 'The best good *Man*, with the Worst natur'd Muse', and Horace Walpole when he described his verses as 'a sort of epigrams'. They are actually an unusual combination of the lyric with the satiric epigram. In form and movement they are true lyrics, but their spirit is that of satire. The most finished of them, the 'Song' beginning 'Dorinda's sparkling wit, and eyes' (see p. 140), is a poem of eight lines, as perfectly finished and proportioned as an epigram of Meleager or Landor. The bold and successful transition from the classical mythology of Cupid in the first stanza of this poem to the realism of the 'black-guard boy' with the link (torch), straight out of the muddy streets of Restoration London, in the second, is sufficient in itself to show that Dorset had a poetic gift of a high order, and to make us regret that he used it so seldom.

Except where another source is indicated, the text of the following poems is that of *The Works of the Most Celebrated Minor Poets, Volume the First*, 1749.

---

[1] See above, p. 37.

Poems by Charles Sackville, Earl of Dorset

To Mr Edward Howard

On his incomparable incomprehensible Poem called

THE BRITISH PRINCES

Come on, you critics, find one fault who dare;
For, read it backward, like a witch's prayer,
'Twill do as well; throw not away your jests
On solid nonsense that abides all tests.
Wit like tierce-claret, when't begins to pall,
Neglected lies, and's of no use at all,
But, in its full perfection of decay
Turns vinegar, and comes again in play.
Thou hast a brain, such as it is indeed;
On what else should thy worm of fancy feed?
Yet in a filbert I have often known
Maggots survive, when all the kernel's gone.
This simile shall stand in thy defence,
'Gainst such dull rogues as now and then write sense.
Thy stile's the same, whatever be thy theme,
As some digestions turn all meat to phlegm.
He lyes, dear Ned, who says thy brain is barren,
Where deep conceits, like vermin breed in carrion.
Thy stumbling founder'd jade can trot as high
As any other Pegasus can fly.
So the dull eel moves nimbler in the mud,
Than all the swift-finn'd racers of the flood.

As skilful divers to the bottom fall,
Sooner than those that cannot swim at all,
So in the way of writing, without thinking,
Thou hast a strange alacrity in sinking.
Thou writ'st below ev'n thy own nat'ral parts,
And with acquired dullness, and new arts
Of study'd nonsense, tak'st kind readers hearts.
Therefore, dear Ned, at my advice, forbear
Such loud complaints 'gainst critics to prefer,
Since thou art turn'd an arrant libeller:
Thou sett'st thy name to what thy self dost write;
Did ever libel yet so sharply bite?

Both this and the following poem are addressed to the Hon. Edward Howard
(b. 1624), fifth son of the Earl of Berkshire. *The British Princes* was a dull and
prolix epic published by Howard in May 1669. He was also the author of
several plays including *The Usurper* (1663/4), *The Change of Crownes* (1667)
and *The Women's Conquest* (1670).

TO THE SAME ON HIS PLAYS

Thou damn'd antipodes to common sense,
Thou foil to Flecknoe,* pr'ythee tell from whence
Does all this mighty stock of dullness spring?
Is it thy own, or hast it from Snow-hill,*
Assisted by some ballad-making quill?
No, they fly higher yet, thy plays are such
I'd swear they were translated out of Dutch.
Fain wou'd I know what diet thou dost keep,
If thou dost always, or dost never sleep?
Sure hasty-pudding is thy chiefest dish,
With bullock's liver, or some stinking fish:
Garbage, ox-cheeks, and tripes, do feast thy brain,
Which nobly pays this tribute back again.
With daizy roots thy dwarfish muse is fed,
A giant's body with a pigmy's head.
Can'st thou not find among thy num'rous race
Of kindred, one to tell thee, that thy plays
Are laught at by the pit, box, galleries, nay, stage?
Think on't a while, and thou wilt quickly find
Thy body made for labour, not thy mind.
No other use of paper thou should'st make,
Than carrying loads and reams about upon thy back.
Carry vast burthens 'till thy shoulders shrink,
But curst be he that gives thee pen and ink:
Such dangerous weapons shou'd be kept from fools,
As nurses from their children keep edged-tools:
For thy dull fancy a muckinder* is fit

2 *Flecknoe:* Richard Flecknoe (d. 1678), a minor poet satirised by Marvell
and Dryden.

4 *Snow-hill:* a narrow, steep highway between Holborn Bridge and Newgate
famous for ballads and ballad-mongers in the time of Charles II.

27 *Muckinder:* the text of 1749 reads 'munkinder'. This is certainly a misprint of muckinder or muckender: a handkerchief.

To wipe the slabberings of thy snotty wit:
And though 'tis late, if justice could be found,
Thy plays like blind-born puppies shou'd be drown'd
For were it not that we respect afford
Unto the son of a heroic lord,
Thine in the ducking-stool shou'd take her seat,
Drest like her self in a great chair of state;
Where, like a muse of quality she'd die,
And thou thy self shalt make her elegy,
In the same strain thou writ'st thy comedy.

SONG

Though, *Phillis*, your prevailing charms
Have forc'd me from my *Celia's* arms,
That kind defence against all powers,
But those resistless eyes of yours:
Think not your conquest to maintain
By rigour and unjust disdain;
In vain, fair Nymph, in vain you strive,
For love does seldom hope survive.
My heart may languish for a time,
Whilst all your Glories in their prime
Can justifie such cruelty
By the same force that conquer'd me.
When age shall come, at whose command
Those troops of Beauty must disband;
A Tyrants strength once took away,
What slave so dull as to obey!

From *A Collection of Poems written upon
Several Occasions by Several Persons* (1672)

SONG

Written at Sea, in the First Dutch War, 1665,
the Night before an Engagement

To all you ladies now at land
    We men at sea indite;
But first wou'd have you understand
    How hard it is to write;
The Muses now, and Neptune too,
We must implore to write to you,
    With a fa, la, la, la, la.

For tho' the Muses should prove kind,
    And fill our empty brain;
Yet if rough Neptune rouze the wind,
    To wave the azure main,
Our paper, pen, and ink, and we,
Roll up and down our ships at sea,
    With a fa, la, la, la, la.

Then, if we write not by each post,
    Think not we are unkind;
Nor yet conclude our ships are lost
    By Dutchmen, or by wind:
Our tears we'll send a speedier way,
The tide shall bring 'em twice a day.
    With a fa, la, la, la, la.

The king with wonder, and surprize,
    Will swear the seas grow bold;
Because the tides will higher rise,
    Then e'er they us'd of old:
But let him know it is our tears
Bring floods of grief to Whitehall stairs.
    With a fa, la, la, la, la.

Should foggy Opdam* chance to know
  Our sad and dismal story;
The Dutch wou'd scorn so weak a foe,
  And quit their fort at Goree:*
For what resistance can they find
From men who've left their hearts behind!
  With a fa, la, la, la, la.

Let wind and weather do its worst,
  Be you to us but kind;
Let Dutchmen vapour, Spaniards curse,
  No sorrow we shall find:
'Tis then no matter how things go,
Or who's our friend, or who's our foe.
  With a fa, la, la, la, la.

To pass our tedious hours away,
  We throw a merry main;
Or else at serious ombre play;
  But, why should we in vain
Each others ruin thus pursue?
We were undone when we left you.
  With a fa, la, la, la, la.

But now our fears tempestuous grow,
  And cast our hopes away;
Whilst you, regardless of our woe,
  Sit careless at a play:
Perhaps permit some happier man
To kiss your hand, or flirt your fan.
  With a fa, la, la, la, la.

29 *Opdam:* Jacob Obdam or Opdam, Dutch Admiral, defeated and killed
in the naval action on 13 June 1665.

32 *Goree:* Island off the West Coast of Africa occupied by the Dutch early
in the seventeenth century.

When any mournful tune you hear,
   That dies in ev'ry note;
As if it sigh'd with each man's care,
   For being so remote;
Think then how often love we've made
To you, when all those tunes were play'd.
   With a fa, la, la, la, la.

In justice you cannot refuse,
   To think of our distress;
When we for hopes of honour lose
   Our certain happiness;
All those designs are but to prove
Ourselves more worthy of your love.
   With a fa, la, la, la, la.

And now we've told you all our loves,
   And likewise all our fears;
In hopes this declaration moves
   Some pity from your tears:
Let's hear of no inconstancy.
We have too much of that at sea.
   With a fa, la, la, la, la.

SONG

Methinks the poor town has been troubled too long,
With Phillis and Chloris in every song;
By fools, who at once can both love and despair,
And will never leave calling 'em cruel and fair;
Which justly provokes me in rhime to express
The truth that I know of bonny black Bess.

This Bess of my heart, this Bess of my soul,
Has a skin white as milk, and hair black as a coal;
She's plump, yet with ease you may span her round waist,
But her round swelling thighs can scarce be embrac'd:
Her belly is soft, not a word of the rest;
But I know what I think, when I drink to the best.

The plowman and 'squire, the arranter clown,
At home she subdu'd in her paragon-gown,*
But now she adorns both the boxes and pit,
And the proudest town-gallants are forc'd to submit;
All hearts fall a leaping wherever she comes,
And beat day and night, like my lord Craven's Drums.*

I dare not permit her to come to Whitehall,
For she'd out-shine the ladies, paint, jewels, and all:
If a lord shou'd but whisper his love in a crowd,
She'd sell him a bargain, and laugh out aloud:
Then the queen over-hearing what Betty did say,
Would send Mr. Roper* to take her away.

14 *paragon-gown:* 'paragon' according to the *O.E.D.* was 'a kind of double camlet, a stuff used for dress and upholstery in the seventeenth and early eighteenth centuries'.

18 *my lord Craven's Drums:* a reference to William Craven, earl of Craven (1606–97), the celebrated champion of the cause of the Queen of Bohemia, who commanded the Coldstream Guards in the reign of Charles II.

24 *Mr Roper:* this is probably Colonel Roper, an English Catholic, who held a position in the household of Queen Catherine of Braganza.

But to those that have had my dear Bess in their arms,
She's gentle, and knows how to soften her charms;
And to every beauty can add a new grace,
Having learn'd how to lisp, and to trip in her pace;
And with head on one side, and a languishing eye,
To kill us by looking as if she would die.

SONG

TO CHLORIS, FROM THE BLIND ARCHER

Ah! Chloris, 'tis time to disarm your bright Eyes,
   And lay by those terrible glances;
We live in an age that's more civil and wise,
   Than to follow the rules of romances.

When once your round bubbies begin but to pout,
   They'll allow you no long time for courting;
And you'll find it a very hard task to hold out;
   For all maidens are mortal at fourteen.

SONG

Phillis, the fairest of love's foes,
   Though fiercer than a dragon,
Phillis, that scorn'd the powder'd beaus,
   What has she now to brag on?
So long she kept her legs so close,
   'Till they had scarce a rag on.

Compell'd thro' want, this wretched maid
   Did sad complaints begin:
Which surly Strephon hearing, said,
   It was both shame and sin,
To pity such a lazy jade,
   As will neither play nor spin.

ON THE COUNTESS OF DORCHESTER,
MISTRESS TO KING JAMES THE SECOND

Written in 1680

Tell me, Dorinda, why so gay,
    Why such embroid'ry, fringe, and lace?
Can any dresses find a way,
To stop th' approaches of decay,
    And mend a ruin'd face?

Wilt thou still sparkle in the box,
    Still ogle in the ring?
Canst thou forget thy age and pox?
Can all that shines in shells and rocks
    Make thee a fine young thing?

So have I seen in larder dark
    Of veal a lucid loin;
Replete with many a brilliant spark,
As wise philosophers remark,
    At once both stink and shine.

SONG

Dorinda's sparkling wit, and eyes,
  United, cast too fierce a light,
Which blazes high, but quickly dies,
  Pains not the heart, but hurts the sight.

Love is a calmer, gentler joy,
  Smooth are his looks, and soft his pace;
Her Cupid is a black-guard boy,
  That runs his link full in your face.

SONG

Sylvia, methinks you are unfit
  For your great lord's embrace;
For tho' we all allow you wit,
  We can't a handsome face.

Then where's the pleasure, where's the good,
  Of spending time and cost?
For if your wit ben't understood,
  Your keeper's bliss is lost.

ON THE SAME

Proud with the spoils of royal cully,
With false pretence to wit and parts,
She swaggers like a batter'd bully,
To try the tempers of mens hearts.

Tho' she appear as glitt'ring fine,
As gems, and jests, and paint can make her;
She ne'er can win a breast like mine;
The devil and Sir David take her.

This and the three preceding poems are all addressed to Katherine Sedley (created countess of Dorchester, 1686), daughter of Sir Charles Sedley and mistress of James II. The lines beginning 'Sylvia, methinks you are unfit' seem to refer to Katherine's remark, when, speaking of herself and James's other mistresses, she is reported to have said: 'We are none of us handsome, and, if we had wit, he has not enough to discern it.' The date '1680' in the title of the lines beginning 'Tell me, Dorinda, why so gay' must be a mistake. Katherine was only twenty-three in 1680 and did not become countess of Dorchester till six years later, 1686, or perhaps 1690, may be the correct reading. The last poem *On the Same* must have been written after 20 August 1696, when Katherine married Sir David Colyear, earl of Portmore (the 'Sir David' mentioned in l. 8).

KNOTTING

At noon, in a sunshiny day,
The brighter lady of the May,
Young Chloris innocent and gay,
   Sat knotting in a shade:

Each slender finger play'd its part,
With such activity and art,
As would inflame a youthful heart,
   And warm the most decay'd.

Her fav'rite swain, by chance, came by
He saw no anger in her eye;
Yet when the bashful boy drew nigh,
   She would have seem'd afraid.

She let her ivory needle fall,
And hurl'd away the twisted ball;
But straight gave Strephon such a call,
   As would have rais'd the dead.

Dear gentle youth, is't none but thee?
With innocence I dare be free;
By so much truth and modesty
   No nymph was e'er betray'd.

Come lean thy head upon my lap;
While thy smooth cheeks I stroke and clap,
Thou may'st securely take a nap;
   Which he, poor fool, obey'd.

She saw him yawn, and heard him snore,
And found him fast asleep all o'er.
She sigh'd, and could endure no more,
   But starting up, she said,

Such virtue shall rewarded be:
For this thy dull fidelity,
I'll trust you with my flocks, not me,
 Pursue thy grazing trade;

Go milk thy goats, and shear thy sheep,
And watch all night thy flocks to keep;
Thou shalt no more be lull'd asleep
 By me mistaken maid.

A PARAPHRASE ON THE FRENCH

In grey-hair'd Cælia's* wither'd arms
    As mighty Lewis lay,
She cry'd, If I have any charms,
    My dearest, let's away.

For you, my love, is all my fear;
    Hark! how the drums do rattle!
Alas, sir! what shou'd you do here
    In dreadful day of battle?

Let little Orange* stay and fight,
    For danger's his diversion;
The wise will think you in the right,
    Not to expose your person:

Nor vex your thoughts how to repair
    The ruins of your glory:
You ought to leave so mean a care
    To those who pen your story.

Are not Boileau and Corneille paid
    For panegyric writing?
They know how heroes may be made,
    Without the help of fighting.

When foes too saucily approach,
    'Tis best to leave them fairly:
Put six good horses to your coach,
    And carry me to Marly.

This poem is an adaptation of some French satirical verses on Louis XIV
and Madame de Maintenon by Madame de La Suze beginning 'La jeune
Iris aux cheveux gris'.

1 *Cælia:* doubtless Madame de Maintenon.

9 *Orange:* William III.

Let Bouflers,* to secure your fame,
   Go take some town, or buy it;
Whilst you, great sir, at Nostredame,
   Te Deum sing in quiet.

25 *Bouflers:* Louis François, duc de Boufflers (1644–1711), Marshal of France, defender of Namur against William III in 1695.

SONG

Phillis, for shame let us improve
   A thousand diff'rent ways,
Those few short moments snatch'd by love,
   From many tedious days.

If you want courage to despise
   The censure of the grave,
Though love's a tyrant in your eyes,
   Your heart is but a slave.

My love is full of noble pride,
   Nor can it e'er submit,
To let that fop, discretion, ride
   In triumph over it.

False friends I have, as well as you,
   Who daily counsel me
Fame and ambition to pursue,
   And leave off loving thee.

But when the least regard I shew
   To fools, who thus advise,
May I be dull enough to grow
   Most miserably wise.

From *A Supplement to the Works of the
Minor Poets*, Part I

ANSWER

Damon, if thou wilt believe me,
'Tis not sighing round the Plain,
Ode, or *Sonnet* can't relieve thee;
Faint attempts in Love are vain.

Love gives out a large Commission
Still Indulgent to the Brave,
But one Sin of base Omission,
Never Woman yet forgave.

Press but home the fair Occasion
And be Master of the Field,
To a Powerful kind Invasion,
Twere a madness not to yield.

Tho' she swears she'll not permit ye,
Crys you're Rude, and much to blame,
Or with tears Implores your Pity;
Be not Merciful for shame,

When the fierce Assault is over,
Cloris soon enough will find,
This her cruel furious Lover,
Much more gentle, not so kind. . . .

From *Poems on Affairs of State*, Part III with other
Miscellany Poems (1698), pp. 198–9

This poem is apparently an answer by Dorset to some sentimental verses by
Jack How printed immediately before it in the same collection. How's poem
begins with the following line: 'Die wretched *Damon*, die quickly to ease her.'

SONG

May the ambitious ever find
　　Success in crouds and noise,
While gentle love does fill my mind
　　With silent real joys,

May knaves and fools grow rich and great,
　　And the world think 'em wise;
While I lie dying at her feet,
　　And all the world despise.

Let conquering kings new triumphs raise,
　　And melt in court delights:
Her eyes can give much brighter days,
　　Her arms much softer nights.

John Wilmot,
Earl of Rochester

. . .he was once one of the greatest of Sinners. *And truly none but one so great in parts could be so; as the chiefest of the Angels for knowledge and power became most degenerate. His sins were like his parts, (for from them corrupted they sprang) all of them high and extraordinary.*

A Sermon Preached At the Funeral of the Rt Honorable John Earl of Rochester By Robert Parsons, M.A., Oxford, 1680

John Wilmot, Earl of Rochester
1647–1680

HE CENTRAL FIGURE of the Restoration Carnival, like the hero of a well-constructed play, did not appear on the stage until the end of the first act. It was not until Christmas Day, 1664, that John Wilmot, second Earl of Rochester, presented himself at the court of Charles II. He was then in his eighteenth year, and was probably one of the handsomest and most accomplished young men in Europe. 'He was a Graceful and well-shaped Person, tall and well made, if not a little too slender: he was exactly well bred, and what by a modest behaviour natural to him, what by a Civility become almost as natural, his Conversation was easie and obliging. He had a strange Vivacity of thought, and vigour of expression: his Wit had a subtility and sublimity both, that were scarce imitable...he had made himself Master of the Ancient and Modern Wit, and of the Modern *French* and *Italian* as well as the *English*.' In addition to this modest and attractive exterior, heredity had provided him with a turbulent and paradoxical character. His father, one of the ablest generals in the Royalist army, had helped Charles II to escape after Worcester and been created earl of Rochester as a reward for his services to the Royal cause. His mother belonged to a famous Puritan family and was a relative of Oliver St John, the great Parliamentary leader. He had been educated at Burford Grammar School and Wadham College, Oxford, where he received the degree of M.A. at the age of fourteen in 1661. In the same year he set out on a 'grand tour' through Europe with Sir Andrew Balfour, a learned Scottish physician whom Charles II had appointed as his tutor. Sir Andrew and his pupil were at Venice, the great pleasure city of that period, in October 1664. At Padua the young earl was enrolled among the 'English nation' at the celebrated university. On his way back he travelled through France, and was entrusted by Henriette, Duchesse d'Orléans, with a letter to her brother Charles II, which he delivered at Whitehall on 25 December 1664. According to Anthony à Wood, the court 'not only debauched' the young Earl but 'made him a perfect Hobbist'. We are told that he was naturally modest, but had already begun to lead a dissipated life when he was at Wadham. The good Dr Balfour had brought 'him back to love Learning and Study', but when he returned to England, and at the age of seventeen was placed in a position of complete independence as a favourite of Charles II in the heady atmosphere of Whitehall, it is not surprising that 'falling into Company that loved these Excesses' he 'blazed out his youth and health in lavish voluptuousness'. Rochester, however, was no mere vulgar debauchee. When Wood writes that he became 'a perfect Hobbist' he is referring to the materialistic philosophy that Rochester learnt from Thomas Hobbes of Malmesbury, who had been tutor to the king and was the fashionable philosopher at the Restoration court. Hobbes taught that there was no such thing as 'soul', 'spirit' or 'mind', and that thought and perception were purely mechanical processes. For him 'good' and 'evil' were merely convenient names with no permanent meaning and no divine sanction: 'Whatsoever is the object of any man's appetite or desire, that is it which he for his part calleth "good", and the object of his hatred and aversion, "evil"; and of his contempt "vile" and "inconsiderable". For these words of good, evil and contemptible, are ever used in relation to the person that useth them, there being nothing simply or absolutely so.' It can easily be imagined that doctrines like these must have been very attractive to a hot-blooded, intelligent young aristocrat brought up by a pious mother in a puritanical household. They seemed to scatter the whole dark cloud of connotation which surrounded such words as 'evil' and 'sin' and to silence the thunders of Sinai for ever. Men would no longer fear a jealous God, but would explain and master the universe by means of the infallible laws of mathematics. Rochester's mind was essentially serious. He made the experiment of living the life of pleasure with an energy and passion equal to that with which men like John Bunyan and George Fox tried to live the life of holiness. 'So confirmed was he in sin', writes Robert Parsons, his mother's chaplain, 'that he lived, and oftentimes almost died, a martyr to it.'

Five months after his appearance at court Rochester caused a sensation by trying to abduct an heiress. The lady was Elizabeth Malet, daughter of a Somersetshire gentleman. Elizabeth was beautiful, witty and accomplished. Her father was dead, and on the death of her mother she was to inherit a fortune yielding an annual income of two thousand five hundred pounds. The king had suggested Rochester as a suitor for her, but her family, represented by Sir John Warre, her step-father, and Lord Hawley, her grandfather, had no desire for her to marry a youth of eighteen with a comparatively new title, and no fortune except his small ancestral estate at Adderley and the pension of five hundred pounds a year granted to him by the king. So the king's proposal was rejected, and the Warres tried to negotiate a marriage with Lord Hinchinbrooke, son of the Earl of Sandwich. Rochester, probably with Elizabeth's consent, then decided to try violent means. On Friday, 26 May 1665, she was supping at Whitehall with Frances Stuart, the king's favourite. Late that night her grandfather (who is described as a 'court buffoon') fetched her in his coach. At Charing Cross they were stopped by a party of armed men. The young lady was placed in another coach, where two women were waiting to receive her. She then disappeared into the night. Rochester probably followed on horseback. Lord Hawley and Sir John Warre promptly appealed to the king. A proclamation was issued on Saturday, the 27th, ordering the apprehension of all who should appear guilty of the misdemeanour. Elizabeth was found soon afterwards and restored to her family. Rochester was imprisoned in the Tower, and from there he addressed a contrite petition to the king ascribing his fault to 'Inadvertency, Ignorance in the Law and Passion'. He was released on 19 June, and soon afterwards volunteered for active service with the fleet against the Dutch. He joined Lord Sandwich's squadron off the Yorkshire coast on 19 July and sailed with it to Bergen, in Norway, where he was present at the attack on the great Dutch East India convoy which had taken refuge in the harbour, and subsequent operations. Sandwich described him in a letter to the king as 'Brave, Industrious, & of parts fitt to be very usefull in yr Matie's service'. It was characteristic of Rochester that during the fighting he tried to test the truth of the doctrine of immortality by experiment. A certain Mr Windham and Edward Montagu, son of Lord Montagu of Boughton, both fellow-volunteers of Rochester, had a presentiment that they would be killed. Windham entered into a solemn engagement with Rochester that, if either of them fell, he would appear and 'give the other notice of the future State, if there was any'. Windham was killed outright and Montagu was mortally wounded and died soon after. The result of the experiment was negative, and the spirit of Windham never returned to give his friend news of the other world. This, Rochester said later, was 'a great snare to him during the rest of his life'. On the other hand, the fulfilment of the presentiment of death felt by both his friends shook his faith in materialism, as it seemed to show that, after all, the soul was something distinct from the body and not merely a name given to the mechanical action of a concourse of atoms.

In the following year Rochester was serving on Sir Edward Spragge's ship in the sanguinary four-day battle between Van Tromp and Monk in the Channel, and was in the thick of the fighting. He went in a small boat under heavy fire to deliver a message from Spragge to one of the other captains and was 'much commended' for this action.' On his return the king made him a present of seven hundred and fifty pounds. Meanwhile Elizabeth Malet had been courted by several wealthy suitors. She seems to have thoroughly enjoyed making fun of these young men who wooed her with one eye on her estate. She toasted one of them, Lord John Butler, in 'a pretty big glasse halfe full of Clarett' and she shocked Lord Hinchinbroke, who was 'not...pleased with the vanity and liberty of her carriage'. It was thought that she might be induced to accept Sir Francis Popham, who, as she said to Mr Ashburnham, 'would kiss her breach to have her'.[1] However, to everyone's surprise, and in defiance of her family's wishes, she chose Rochester, who married her on 20 January 1666/7. The king, we are told, was 'very well satisfyed' and Sir John Warre and Lord Hawley were doubtless furious. Elizabeth might have fared worse. With all his faults Rochester was not a fortune-hunter. He never seems to have touched a penny of his wife's fortune. In one of his letters to her he writes that he is rendering 'an Account of y^r entire revenue, wch I will bee bound to say has hithertoo, and shall (as long as I can gett bread without itt) bee wholly imploy'd to the use of y^r self and those who depend on you'.

In March 1667, Rochester was appointed a gentleman of the king's bedchamber with an annual salary of one thousand pounds, and in June he received a commission as captain in

[1] See Pepys's Diary s.d. 26 Aug. and 25 Nov. 1666.

Prince Rupert's Horseguards. On 29 July he took his seat in the House of Lords, and on 30 August his first child, Anne, was baptised. On 28 February he was appointed gamekeeper of the county of Oxford. His marriage and the offices which he held do not seem to have interfered in any way with his experiment of living the life of pleasure and excitement to the full. Burnet writes that 'the natural heat of his fancy, being inflamed by Wine, made him so extravagantly pleasant, that many to be more diverted by that humor, studied to engage him deeper and deeper in Intemperance: which at length did so entirely subdue him; that, as he told me, for five years together he was continually Drunk; not all the while under the visible effect of it, but his blood was so inflamed that he was not in all that time cool enough to be perfectly Master of himself. This led him to say many wild and unaccountable things....' He was one of the leading spirits in the very fast set called the Ballers, who met at the house of Mrs Bennett, the notorious procuress, and disported themselves with her 'ladies'. His conduct at court and the indulgence shown to him by Charles II shocked many observers. On 16 February 1668/9, the king, with Rochester and other courtiers, was present at a dinner given to the Dutch ambassadors. Rochester, offended by some 'mirth and raillery' of Tom Killigrew, gave him 'a box on the ear in the king's presence'. Charles not only pardoned him but the next day 'did publickly walk up and down, and Rochester... with him as free as ever'. Soon afterwards Rochester seems to have insulted Killigrew's father and this time the king did not forgive him so easily. The atmosphere of Whitehall was growing too hot for him, and in March he went to Paris, carrying a letter from the king to his beloved sister, Henriette d'Orléans. 'This bearer, my lord Rochester', wrote Charles, 'has a mind to make a little journey to Paris, and would not kiss your hands without a letter from me; Pray use him as one I have a very

good opinion of.' He was still in Paris in July. Early in that
month he was at the Opera with Lord William Cavendish
and some other Englishmen, when they were attacked by
some drunken French officers. Louis XIV had the offenders
imprisoned, but Rochester and Cavendish generously
pleaded on their behalf and they were released. On 15 July,
Montagu, the English ambassador in Paris, wrote to ask
permission for Rochester to return. This request seems to
have been granted, as Rochester was in London again in
November, when he was challenged to a duel by a conceited
young nobleman called John Sheffield, earl of Mulgrave.[1]
Sheffield thought Rochester had spread a malicious report
about him 'according to his custom', and he sent Colonel
Aston to him with a challenge. Rochester proved that he was
quite innocent of the offence imputed to him and Mulgrave
declared himself satisfied with his explanation. However, this
was a question of 'honour', and 'honour' could be satisfied
only by fighting. The situation seems to have appealed to
Rochester's sense of humour. He demanded that the combatants should fight on horseback, and it was arranged that they
should meet in some fields near Knightsbridge. Mulgrave
and his second, Aston, after spending the night at a miserable
tavern, met Rochester at the appointed rendezvous. He was
attended not by his friend George Porter, whom he had
named as his second, but by an 'errant life-guardsman'.
Rochester and the life-guardsman were well mounted, whereas Mulgrave and Aston had only 'a couple of pads'. It was
therefore decided that the duel should be on foot after all,
and Mulgrave and Rochester went into an adjoining field to
fight. When they reached the chosen spot Rochester, according to Mulgrave's account, declared that he was not in

[1] I follow the account of this affair given by Sheffield in his *Memoirs*.
Entries in the *Journals of the House of Lords* (vol. XII, pp. 272-7) show
that the duel was actually stopped by the intervention of the King.

a fit state of health to fight, and positively refused to go on with the farce. Mulgrave solemnly called up the seconds to witness the conditions on which the duel was abandoned, 'in order to spread everywhere the true reason for our returning without having fought', and he writes that Rochester's reputation for courage was 'entirely ruined, tho' nobody had still a greater as to wit'. The truth of the matter is probably that Rochester, who was no more a coward than Falstaff, thoroughly enjoyed the fun of dragging the haughty Mulgrave and his second out to Knightsbridge on a fool's errand, and that his chief object was to ridicule the contemporary notions of 'honour' and the absurd convention of duelling. From this time onward Sheffield was Rochester's enemy and much of the scandal which has hung round Rochester's reputation is probably due to reports spread by him. Pope told his friend Spence that 'Lord Rochester was of a very bad turn of mind as well as debauched' and he said that he had his information from 'The Duke of Buckingham (Sheffield) and others who knew him'.

Numerous stories were told of Rochester's witty sayings and his wild pranks. Some of them are undoubtedly apocryphal and others certainly authentic. There is no reason to doubt the authenticity of the celebrated extempore quatrain which he is said to have composed on Charles II. The most reliable version of the story is that preserved by Thomas Hearne, the antiquary, who was a friend of one of Rochester's tutors. According to Hearne, 'on occasion of his Majestie's saying he would leave every one to his liberty in talking, when himself was in company, and would not take what was said at all amiss', Rochester composed the following lines:

> We have a pretty witty king
> 　　Whose word no man relys on:
> He never said a foolish thing,
> 　　And never did a wise one.

Charles's good-humoured reply was that what Rochester observed was easily explained. He was responsible for his words, but his ministers for his actions. This epigram, however, is mild compared with some of the longer lampoons on the king which have been ascribed to Rochester. The character of Charles II seems to have fascinated him, perhaps because, like his own, it was full of paradoxes. The contrast between the old conception of the monarch hedged in by 'divinity' and the actual person of the 'sauntering', informal, pleasure-loving Charles Stuart was a never-failing source of ironic amusement to the poet. What seemed to Rochester especially despicable was not so much that the king amused himself with women but that he allowed himself to be governed by them:

> Restless he rolls about from Whore to Whore,
> A Merry Monarch, scandalous and poor.

The satire in which these lines occur is one of several of which the story is told that a copy became mixed by accident with Charles's papers and that he drew it out of his pocket in the presence of a large company at court. Rochester seems to have taken an impish delight in circulating witty and malicious lampoons. According to Burnet, he employed a footman who 'knew all the court' to act as his spy and to obtain materials for his satiric poems: 'He furnished him with a red coat and a musket as a centinel, and kept him all the winter long every night at the doors of such ladies as he believed might be in intrigues. In the Court a centinel is little minded, and is believed to be posted by a captain of the guards to hinder a combat: so this man saw who walked about and visited at forbidden hours.... By this means Lord Rochester made many discoveries. And when he was well furnished with materials, he used to retire to the country for a month or two to write libels.' Another person whom he

employed to obtain information concerning the secrets of the
court ladies was a pretty girl called Sarah Cooke, who was
employed by the duchess of York. Later Rochester is said
to have trained her for the stage and she became 'one of the
prettiest but one of the worst actresses in the kingdom'. A
more famous actress than Sarah Cooke owed her first success
on the stage to Rochester. This was Elizabeth Barry, one of
the most celebrated of Restoration actresses. She is said to
have been originally a servant of a Lady Shelton in Norfolk.
Rochester 'entered into a Wager, that by proper Instruction,
in less than six Months he would engage she should be the
finest Player on the Stage'. He took immense trouble in
teaching her 'not only the proper cadence or sounding of the
voice, but to seize also the passions, and adapt her whole
behaviour to the situations of the character'. The girl, who
'at the age of fifteen could neither sing nor dance, no, not even
a Country-Dance', was thus engaged by the Duke's Company in 1674. Her first appearance was a complete failure;
and she was dismissed at the end of the season. Rochester
refused, however, to admit defeat and made further efforts
to develop his pupil's talents. Probably through his influence
she was re-engaged in the following year and played the part
of Draxilla in Otway's *Alcibiades* (1675) with great success.
Her subsequent career was brilliant and she became one of
the most popular English actresses of the late seventeenth
and early eighteenth centuries, acting leading parts in plays
by Dryden, Otway, Lee, Vanbrugh, Congreve and others.
She was not beautiful, but her appearance was striking; 'in
characters of greatness' she had a presence of 'elevated
dignity', and in comedy was 'alert, easy and genteel'. She had
a daughter by Rochester, born in November 1677, and it may
well be that his beautiful lines beginning 'Leave this gawdy
guilded stage' (see p. 193) are addressed to her.

Nothing has injured Rochester's reputation more than the

charge, commonly repeated by nineteenth-century critics, that he treated contemporary men of letters harshly and tyrannically. He has been accused of favouring Settle and Crowne at the expense of Dryden and of instigating the brutal outrage called 'The Rose Alley Ambuscade', in which Dryden was attacked and cudgelled by three ruffians in Rose Alley, Covent Garden, on 18 December 1679. There is no real evidence to support any of these allegations, and it has now been shown that Rochester is almost certainly innocent of the last and most serious offence. Settle's 'heroic' tragedy, *The Empress of Morocco*, was performed at court in the spring of 1671/2 with prologues by Rochester and his enemy Mulgrave. It has been said that Rochester obtained for Settle this honour which had not hitherto been granted to Dryden. There is no reason, however, to doubt Settle's own statement that the court production was due to the influence of the Earl of Norwich. At any rate, about a year later Rochester seems to have been on excellent terms with Dryden, who dedicated to him his fine comedy *Marriage à la Mode*, staged at the Duke's Theatre in May 1672, and published in 1673. In his dedication Dryden states explicitly that Rochester drew the King's attention to the merits of his play, and vindicated his writings from the censure of his enemies. He also acknowledges the debt which his comedy owed to Rochester's brilliant conversation. Rochester seems to have written to Dryden to thank him for the dedication, and Dryden replied in a charming letter, written in the summer of 1673, giving all the gossip of the town to the earl, who was in the country at the time. The interruption of the pleasant relations between the two great poets of the Restoration is one of the tragedies of literary history. It seems that Dryden's rather humdrum and colourless character annoyed Rochester, just as Wordsworth's dull respectability infuriated Byron in a later age. Rochester's view was that a poet should be a poet through and through and not a man undistinguished in any way except for a prodigious facility in the making of verses. He expressed this opinion in his *Allusion to Horace*, a witty and penetrating review of contemporary writers, written probably in the winter of 1675/6. In this poem he admits Dryden's greatness:

> Nor dare I from his sacred Temples tear
> That *Lawrel*, which he best deserves to wear.

But he is angry with the Laureate for prostituting his talents by turning himself into a sort of machine for the production of smooth verses to order:

> Five hundred Verses ev'ry *Morning* writ,
> Proves you no more a *Poet*, than a *Wit*.

An additional cause of offence was certainly the fact that Dryden had allied himself closely with Rochester's enemy Mulgrave. It is probable that a rather bitter passage in the Preface to Dryden's *Marriage à la Mode* published in 1678 is an answer to Rochester's criticism. Without mentioning names, Dryden here glances at those who want 'to distinguish themselves from the Herd of Gentlemen by their Poetry' and who write 'malicious Satyr' on poor poets. Writing to his friend Henry Savile in an undated letter from Woodstock, Rochester refers to his quarrel with Dryden: 'You give me word, That I am out of favour with a certain Poet, whom I have ever admir'd for the disproportion of him and his Attributes: He is a Rarity which I cannot but be fond of, as one would be of a Hog that could fiddle, or a singing Owl. If he falls on me at the Blunt, which is his very good Weapon in Wit, I will forgive him, if you please and leave the Repartee to Black Will, with a Cudgel.' The last words in this passage have been commonly quoted as proof that Rochester was responsible for the cudgelling of Dryden in December

1679. Professor J. H. Wilson, however, has shown that the letter in which the words occur was written in April 1676, so it is certain that they had no connection with the Rose Alley affair. The view of Dryden expressed in this letter is very similar to that which is found in *The Allusion to the Tenth Satyre of Horace*. Rochester is writing in a light vein and the reference to Black Will and the cudgel is either merely a joke or a literary allusion which could be understood only by someone with an intimate knowledge of Restoration court gossip. In a letter to Savile dated 21 November 1679, Rochester mentions 'a Libel, in which my share is not the least'. The libel is Mulgrave's *Essay on Satyr* which was being circulated at that time. It contains a long, malicious 'character' of Rochester. The author professes to despise him for 'mere lack of Wit', but his great fault, according to Mulgrave, was that he was no fighting man:

> For (there's the folly that's still mix't with fear)
> Cowards more blows than any Hero bear;
> Of fighting sparks, fame may her pleasure say,
> But 'tis a bolder thing to run away.

The whole passage is full of the hatred of the man with a narrow, conventional mind for a bold and original thinker. The *Essay* was commonly attributed to Dryden and it is likely that he revised Mulgrave's work. The real perpetrator of the Rose Alley outrage, as Antony à Wood and Narcissus Luttrell suspected, was probably Louise de Kéroualle, countess of Portsmouth, the king's French mistress, a jealous and vindictive woman who was described in the wittiest passage in the poem (together with the duchess of Cleveland) as

> False, foolish, old, ill-natur'd and ill-bred.

Rochester may well have deliberately courted the king's anger sometimes in order to have an excuse for leaving Whitehall and satisfying his hunger for variety and adventure. He was certainly a born actor and he seems to have delighted in devising pranks which gave him an opportunity to use his histrionic talent. We are told that he 'took pleasure to disguise himself, as a *Porter*, or as a *Beggar*; sometimes to follow some mean Amours, which for the variety of them, he affected; at other times, meerly for diversion, he would go about in odd shapes in which he acted his part so naturally, that even those who were in the secret, and saw him in these shapes, could perceive nothing by which he might be discovered'.

Rochester's most famous picaresque exploit was the occasion of one of the most amusing of his writings. In June 1676, he was involved in a drunken brawl at Epsom with Etherege and others.[1] This was the scuffle in which Mr Downs, one of the 'merry gang' received his death wound. It was probably as a result of this affair that Rochester was exiled from the court, and he seems to have told his friends that he was going to France. Accompanied, however, by his servant, Thomas Alcock, he went no farther than Tower Hill, where he took lodgings and set up as a quack doctor under the name of Alexander Bendo. He dressed for the part 'in an old overgrown green gown which he religiously wore in memory of Rabelais his master, put on at the reception of his doctor's degree at Montpellier, lined through with exotick furs of diverse colours, an antique cap, a great reverend beard and a magnificent medal set round with glittering pearl, rubies and diamond... hung about his neck in a massy gold-like chain which he said the King of Cyprus had given him'. Dr Bendo, in the manner of contemporary charlatans, issued a bill which is a little masterpiece, worthy of Swift. In it he claims to cure a large variety of diseases, beginning with 'the *Labes Britanica*, or Grand *English* Disease, the *Scurvy*', and proceeding by way of 'Gouts, Aches, Dropsies and Con-

[1] See above, p. 81.

sumptions' to 'Green-Sickness, Weaknesses, Inflammations, or Obstructions in the Stomach, Reins, Liver, Spleen, etc.' He also professes that, without destroying the complexion of women, he can 'render them purely Fair, clearing and preserving them from all Spots, Freckles, Heats, and Pimples, any Marks of the Small-Pox'.

'Dr Bendo's' ingenious plea that he is all the more likely to be a 'true Man' because he looks like a 'counterfeit' may be quoted as an example both of Rochester's ironic wit and of his mastery of the 'other harmony' of prose:

'However, *Gentlemen*, in a World like this (where Virtue is so exactly Counterfeited, and Hypocrisie so generally taken notice of, that every one, arm'd with Suspicions, stands upon his Guard against it) 'twill be very hard for a Stranger especially, to escape a Censure.

'All I shall say for my self on this Score is this: If I appear to any one like a Counterfeit, ev'n for the sake of that chiefly, ought I to be construed a true Man, who is the Counterfeits Example, his Original, and that which he employs his Industry and Pains to imitate and copy: Is it therefore my fault, if the Cheat by his Wits and Endeavours makes himself so like me that consequently I cannot avoid resembling of him? Consider, pray, the Valiant and the Coward; the wealthy Merchant and the Bankrupt; the Politician and the Fool; they are the same in many things, and differ but in *one* alone. The Valiant Man holds up his Head, looks confidently round about him, wears a Sword, courts a Lord's Wife, and owns it: So does the Coward; one only Point of Honour, and that's Courage, (which, like false Metal, one only Trial can discover) makes the distinction.

'The Bankrupt walks the *Exchange*, buys Bargains, draws Bills and accepts them with the richest, whilst Paper and Credit are current Coin: That which makes the difference, is real Cash, a great Defect indeed, and yet but one, and that the last to be found out, and 'till then the least perceiv'd.

'Now for the Politician, he is a grave deliberating, close, prying Man: Pray, are there not grave, deliberating, close, prying Fools? If then the Difference betwixt all these (though infinite in effect) be so nice in all appearance, will you expect it should be otherwise betwixt the false Physician, Astrologer, &c. and the true? The first calls himself Learned Doctor, sends forth his Bills, gives Physick and Counsel, tells and foretels; the other is bound to do just as much; 'tis only your Experience must distinguish betwixt them; to which I willingly submit my self; I'll only say something to the Honour of the Mountebank, in case you discover me to be one.

'Reflect a little what kind of Creature 'tis: He is one then who is fain to supply some higher Ability he pretends to, with Craft: He draws great Companies to him, by undertaking strange things which can never be effected.

'The Politician (by his Example, no doubt) finding how the People are taken with specious, miraculous Impossibilities, plays the same Game, protests, declares, promises I know not what things, which he's sure can ne'er be brought about: The people believe, are deluded, and pleas'd, the Expectation of a future Good, which shall never befal them, draws their Eyes off of a present Evil. Thus are *They* kept and establish'd in Subjection, Peace, and Obedience; *He* in Greatness, Wealth, and Power: So you see the *Politician* is, and must be a *Mountebank* in State-Affairs, and the Mountebank (no doubt if he thrives) is an arrant *Politician* in Physick.'

The 'Doctor' gave advice gratis, but his numerous clients paid for his remedies (concocted from ground brick, slate, soot, ashes, soap and nastier things) in 'good gold and silver' with 'thanks to boot'. Some ladies were too modest to visit Dr Bendo. Rochester, with the aid of a tirewoman, used to assume the dress of a grave matron and visit these fastidious persons in their own apartments. When 'the hungry court could sustain her drooping spirits no longer' he surprised his friends who thought he was in exile on the Continent by appearing one night at a ball at Whitehall 'in as great favour as ever and nobody knew what had become of the Mountebanks' or guessed who they were until long afterwards.

The year 1676 may, perhaps, be reckoned as the culminating point of Rochester's career as the most brilliant and original of the wits of the Restoration court. In the spring of that year Gentle George Etherege produced his finest comedy, *Sir Fopling Flutter or The Man of Mode*, with Dorimant, who is certainly a portrait of Rochester, as its hero. Dorimant is a picture of Rochester in his prime, equally at ease whether he is talking brilliantly to his friends the wits, paying compliments to fine ladies, rallying an absurd, affected mistress of a conceited fop, or bandying jests with an orangewoman and a shoemaker. Etherege reveals the true significance of his character when he shows him dressing in the height of fashion and at the same time capable of perceiving the absurdity of dandyism: 'That a man's excellency should lie in neatly tying of a Ribbond, or a Crevat.'

Already the life of the complete hedonist, into which he had flung himself with such ardour, had begun to pall. For some years he had been writing satires in which he tears the glittering veil from the Restoration pageant and shows the ugliness and squalor that lay behind it. In *A Letter from Artemisa in the Town to Cloe in the Country* he make his heroine, after her bitter sketch of the harlot Corinna, assure her friend that she knows as many more stories of the same kind

> As joyn'd to these, shall to a Volume swell;
> As true as Heav'n, more infamous than Hell.

Sometimes, disgusted with the pettiness and stupidity of the court, he would retire to his estates and live the life of a country gentleman in Oxfordshire and Somersetshire. Strangely enough, the celebrated libertine and scoffer of Whitehall and Covent Garden was an affectionate husband and father and a popular and energetic landlord. His letters to his wife, full of domestic details, references to presents sent from London, commissions which she had entrusted to him and messages to the children, are delightfully humorous and tender. He used to say 'when he came to Brentford the devill entred into him and never left him till he came to the country again to Adderbury or Woodstock'. He took his duties as a landlord seriously. In August 1670, we find him at the head of a number of gentlemen whose manors adjoined the Chase of Kingswood, in Gloucestershire, petitioning the king against a certain Sir Baynham Throckmorton, who had obtained a lease of sixty years of all the king's rights and oppressed the commoners and cottagers. This action shows that Rochester had a sense of the responsibilities attached to his rank, and it accords ill with the traditional picture of the heartless court fribble. At any rate, his neighbours in the West seem to have trusted him. On 30 October 1672, he was appointed deputy lieutenant of Somerset, and in November 1677, he was elected an alderman of Taunton. He also held various offices in his own county of Oxford. He had been appointed gamekeeper of the county in 1668. The posts that he coveted, however, were those of keeper and ranger of the royal hunting forest of Woodstock, near his ancestral estate. The two offices were granted to Lord Lovelace on 2 November 1674, but on the 27th of the following February the grant was revoked in so far as it concerned the rangership, which was given to Rochester, and on 2 May he was appointed to the keepership as well. One of Rochester's objects in seeking these two posts was doubtless to obtain possession of the pretty old hunting-box called the High Lodge at the west end of the forest, which was the Ranger's official residence. The High Lodge commands one of the finest views in Oxfordshire over the great forest walk which runs between magnificent groves of oaks stretching towards the distant blue Cotswolds. Here he could find peace and quiet among his books, and here, we are told, he could often spend 'some months wholly imployed in Study or Sallies of his Wit'. He decorated the old lodge according to his taste and is said to have had 'several lascivious pictures drawen there'. He used to receive his friends at the High Lodge, and Buckingham, Buckhurst, Shepherd and Savile were frequent visitors. In October 1677, Buckingham promised to wait on him at Woodstock 'with the best pack of hounds that ever ran upon English ground'.

Rochester's health, which had never been robust, declined steadily from about 1671 onwards. He had contracted a venereal disease early in life, and he also appears to have been consumptive. In September 1671, he suddenly walked out of Garraway's Coffee-House, where he was dining with some of his friends, and posted down to the country, where he suffered much from pain in the eyes. After the winter of 1676/7 he seems to have regained his health for only comparatively short periods. He was ill in the spring of 1677, but in August he was well enough to be in town and the king and Buckingham were 'very merry' one evening at his lodgings. In the autumn he was ill again, and in October he wrote to Savile that he was 'almost Blind, utterly Lame and scarce within hopes of ever seeing London again'. Yet he was able to carry on a witty correspondence with his old friend, whom he praises for loving 'a Man whom it is the great Mode to hate'. In the winter of 1677/8 he appears to have had a very severe relapse.

It was still possible to escape from the nightmare of boredom and despair by plunging into dissipation. He could call for louder music and for stronger wine. It was possible, but it was becoming increasingly difficult. The Restoration Carnival was turning into a horrible *danse macabre*, a ballet of sinister and grotesque figures:

> Mishapen Monsters round in Measures went
> Horrid in Form with Gestures insolent;
> Grinning throu Goatish Beards with half clos'd Eyes.[1]

A fragment of a letter addressed to his wife contains one of his most self-revealing statements; '...so great a disproportion t'wixt our desires and what is ordained to content them; but you will say this is pride and madness, for there are those soe intirely satisfyed with theire shares in this world that theire wishes nor theire thoughts have not a farther prospect of felicity & glory.' The philosophy of Hobbes on which he built his life of self-indulgence led to complete egoism:

> In my dear self, I center ev'rything,
> My *Servants*, *Friends*, my *Mistress* and my *King*,
> Nay Heav'n and *Earth*, to that one poynt I bring.[2]

Yet this egoism produced only boredom and contempt for all mankind with no 'prospect of felicity & glory' which could bring him lasting contentment. This was the mood in which he composed his greatest poem, the *Satyr Against Mankind*, written before 23 March 1675/6, and published anonymously in June 1679. It represents the end of the cul-de-sac into which the philosophy of hedonism had led him, a blank

---

[1] These lines are spoken by Lucina, the heroine of Rochester's tragedy *Valentinian* (4to, 1685), Act III, sc. iii.

[2] From Rochester's poem entitled *A very Heroical Epistle in Answer to Ephelia*, ll. 7–9. (See *Poems by John Wilmot, Earl of Rochester*, ed. V. de S. Pinto, p. 43.)

wall of misanthropy, and a renunciation of the belief in 'reason':

> 'Tis this very reason I despise,
> This supernatural gift that makes a *Myte*,
> Think he is the Image of the Infinite.

Later in the poem he concedes that there is nothing wrong with reason if it is rightly used, but he launches into a new onslaught on Man, whom he now attacks not merely for being miserable and absurd but for his baseness and inhumanity to his fellows:

> Be Judge your self, I'le bring it to the test,
> Which is the basest *Creature*, *Man*, or *Beast*?
> *Birds* feed on *Birds*, *Beasts* on each other Prey,
> But Savage *Man* alone, does *Man*, betray.

It is significant that here Rochester implicitly rejects the egoistic immoralism which he had hitherto flaunted. In a curious epilogue added in some editions to *A Satyr Against Mankind* he makes a sort of conditional recantation. He is seeking for a man whom he can admire:

> A meek humble Man of modest sense,
> Who Preaching peace does practice continence;
> Whose pious life's a proof he does believe
> Misterious truths which no Man can conceive.

He ends the epilogue by offering to 'recant his "Paradox"' if 'such Godlike Men' can be found, but even if he is convinced of the existence of really good men he will still retain his former opinion of the rest and his conclusion will be that

> *Man* differs more from *Man*, than *Man* from *Beast*.

He had begun to see that he must retreat from the blind alley of materialistic hedonism and find a new philosophy of life if he were to achieve the 'felicity & glory' of which he had written to his wife.

It was in the summer of 1678 that Rochester first heard of Gilbert Burnet, afterwards bishop of Salisbury, but at this time a young Scottish clergyman whose preaching had attracted much attention, and who had recently been appointed a royal chaplain. Burnet was attending on a dying lady who had 'been engaged in a criminal amour' with Rochester. During his convalescence Rochester read and enjoyed the first volume of Burnet's *History of the Reformation*, which had just appeared. They met accidentally two or three times, and in October 1679, Burnet heard from a gentleman of his acquaintance that Rochester who was then recovering from a severe illness, wanted to see him. After a few visits a genuine friendship sprang up between these two very different characters, the brilliant young English peer who had been the cynosure of a dissolute court and the austere, hard-working Scottish parson who had spent most of his time among his books or in the pulpit. A link which bound them together was their common delight in intellectual argument and philosophic speculation. In Burnet Rochester found a priest of a kind that he had never met before, a disinterested seeker after truth with a genuine interest in philosophy instead of a mere mouthpiece for traditional piety. Burnet gained his confidence to such an extent that Rochester told him he would treat him 'with more freedom than he had ever used to men of my [Burnet's] Profession'. He gave Burnet a 'full view' of his life and they agreed to enter into a regular debate on religion and morality. This debate, in spite of the fact that Rochester was 'in a low state of health', continued throughout the winter of 1679-80. At the same time, Rochester was in communication with Charles Blount, son of Sir Henry Blount, who was recognised at that time as one of the leaders of the English deists or freethinkers who rejected revealed religion and accepted the 'five points' of Lord Herbert of Cherbury, the father of deism or 'natural religion'. Rochester seems to have made Blount's acquaintance in the winter of 1678 and they had some discussion on the subject of religion during the winter. Early in 1680 Rochester saw the deist again and they talked about the nature of the soul and immortality. In February Rochester sent him his fine poem on Death, based on a passage in the *Troades* of Seneca. During that winter it seems that Blount the deist and Burnet the Christian were wrestling for Rochester's soul. Blount's arguments are what we should now call Voltairian. His object seems to be to show that Christian orthodoxy was the invention of cunning priests who could impose on the credulity of ignorant people. He tries to turn on to the sacred traditions of Europe the dry, hard light of the Enlightenment, but his arguments are feeble, and he is no match for Burnet as a logician. In reply to a request from Rochester he sent him a Latin fragment of his father, Sir Henry Blount, on the nature of the soul. He describes the views expressed in this fragment as 'twilight conjectures'. He admits that there is a divine element in the world—τὸ θεῖον or 'Divinum Aliquid'—but he argues that men are incapable of discerning it 'so that (indeed) all Philosophy excepting Scepticism is mere dotage'. Here indeed is a confession of failure. 'Scepticism' could no longer satisfy Rochester and the arid creed of deism gave him no real contact with the 'Divinum Aliquid', which was what he was really seeking.

Burnet after his fashion was as much a child of the Enlightenment as was Blount, and the Christianity which he expounded to Rochester was in essentials the rationalised philosophic religion of his master, John Smith and the Cambridge Platonists. The miraculous and mythical elements in Christianity are explained away as allegories or dismissed as unimportant. In place of the 'natural God' of the deists, we have a God who is good and rational, or in other words a deification of those concepts. Little stress is laid on 'the business of the Fall of Man' and 'other things of which we cannot perhaps give our selves a perfect account'. Christianity is a way of life to be judged 'by the Rules it gives, and the Methods it prescribes'. Its keystone is the golden rule of the Gospels 'Of doing as we would have others do to us, and loving our Neighbours as ourselves'. A sharp distinction is to be drawn between 'Truths about the Divine Essence of which the manner is not understood', and such an alleged 'mystery' as transubstantiation of which Burnet speaks as contemptuously as any deist. The Christianity which Burnet expounded to Rochester is the religion of the latitudinarians: 'Christianity not Mysterious.' The conference ended with an admission by Rochester of the anti-social character of libertinism: 'Vice and Impiety were as contrary to Humane society as Wild Beasts let loose would be.' He announced his firm intention 'to change the whole method of his Life'. Intellectually he was convinced by Burnet's arguments in favour of Christian ethics. He had not yet arrived 'at a full persuasion of Christianity', but he 'would never employ his Wit more to run it down or corrupt others'. The conversations ended in the spring of 1680. He left London in April 1680, intending to follow his usual practice of spending the summer in the country. His health seemed much improved and he attended the Newmarket races. After his return from Newmarket he decided to visit his wife's estates in Somerset and 'rode thither post'. The exertion proved too much for him and he arrived at Enmore in a state of collapse. He was brought back by coach with great difficulty to his favourite house, the High Lodge in Woodstock Forest. Throughout the summer he lay in agony in the great four-poster bed in the room overlooking the green forest and the distant Cotswolds. His anguish was mental as well as physical. He was overcome by a frenzy of

remorse for his past life and a disgust with everything connected with it, 'a most penetrating cutting Sorrow'.

He was nursed by his wife and his mother, and several
clergymen, including the bishop of Oxford, visited him. He
took most pleasure in the ministrations of a young man called
Robert Parsons, his mother's chaplain. His deliverance from
mental agony came to him one day when Parsons was reading
to him the noble poetry of the 'Second Isaiah' describing the
Suffering Servant of Yahweh:

> ...he shall grow up before him as a tender plant,
> And as a root out of a drie ground:
> Hee hath no forme nor comelinesse.
> And when wee shall see him, there is no beautie
>   that we should desire him.
> He is despised and rejected of men,
> A man of sorrows, and acquainted with griefe:
> And we hid as it were our faces from him;
> Hee was despised and wee esteemed him not.
>
> He shall see of the travell of his soule, and shall be satisfied;
> By his knowledge shall my righteous servant justifie many:
> For hee shall bear their iniquities....

When Rochester heard these words of the Hebrew prophet
in the noble English of the Authorised Version he felt at last
that significant emotion for which he had been longing and
knew in a flash by direct experience the 'Divinum Aliquid'
which he had sought vainly among the deists and which even
Burnet's rational Christianity had failed to reveal to him.
His great moment of illumination can only be described in
his own words: 'as he heard it [the passage from Isaiah] read,
he felt an inward force upon him, which did so enlighten his
Mind and convince him, that he could resist it no longer. For
the words had an authority which did shoot like Raies or

Beams in his Mind; so that he was not only convinced by the Reasonings he had about it, which satisfied his Understanding, but by a power which did so effectually constrain him, that he did ever after firmly believe in his Saviour, as if he had seen him in the clouds.' There is no doubt that this is a description of a genuine mystical experience. Rochester describes it by means of the metaphor of an energising light, the image commonly used by intellectual mystics whose minds work with concepts instead of pictorial images.

The date of this 'conversion' was probably 19 June. Rochester did nothing by halves. On the same day he made a kind of public recantation, calling in all his servants, including even the 'piggard boy' or lad who looked after the swine. Before them all he read and signed a declaration expressing abhorrence of his past life and warning all against denying God or making a mock of sin or religion. This document was witnessed by his mother and Robert Parsons. Then he took the sacrament with his wife, who, to his great joy, had renounced Roman Catholicism, to which she had been converted partly at his own instigation. It was probably on this day, too, that he gave strict orders to burn all his 'profane and lewd writings . . . and all his obscene and filthy pictures'. When this holocaust took place, a manuscript, 'History of the Intrigues of the Court of Charles II, in a series of letters to his friend Henry Savile', was apparently overlooked, but unfortunately this book, which must have been one of his most interesting works, was burnt by his mother after his death. Just as he had once flung himself heart and soul into the life of pleasure and fashion so now he would plunge with equal ardour into the life of sanctity. The experiment of Hobbes had failed; he would now attempt the experiment of Pascal. He told Parsons that, if he lived, he would make it his business to try to produce 'an Idea of Divine Poetry', and it is probable that two poems, *Plain Dealings Downfall* and

Consideratus Considerandus,[1] ascribed to him in one of the editions published soon after his death, represent a first attempt to carry out this resolution. The central image of both is that of virtue conceived as poor, homeless, rejected and outcast. Both seem to be connected with the description of the Suffering Servant in Isaiah liii, which, Parsons tells us in his Funeral Sermon on Rochester, the Earl got by heart. His tragedy was that his body was too enfeebled for him to give adequate artistic expression to his new experience. Indeed, he had only a month of life before him. He wrote to Burnet to tell him about his conversion and to ask him to come to the High Lodge, but Burnet did not realise the seriousness of his condition and reached his bedside only on 20 July. He lived for six days after Burnet's arrival. Sometimes his thoughts went back to the past and he spoke with great affection of his old tutor, Sir Andrew Balfour, of whom Burnet's Scottish accent probably reminded him. Early on the 25th Burnet had to depart. 'Has my friend left me?' he said. 'Then I shall die shortly.' After that he spoke only once or twice more, but lay for the most part in silence. Once he was heard praying devoutly. At two o'clock in the morning on 26 July 1680, the last flicker of life went out of the wasted body, 'without any *Convulsion*, or so much as a groan'

Rochester was the one great poet among the Restoration wits, an eagle among butterflies. His reputation has suffered from the blaze of notoriety which surrounded his life and character and also from the fact that much scurrilous and obscene trash by other writers was fathered on to him by dishonest editors after his death. He could play the game of the rococo pastoral in verse with exquisite grace when he wanted to, and some of his lyrics are masquerades in the Dresden china manner of Sarrazin, Voiture, Waller and Sedley.

[1] See below, pp. 209, 210.

Rochester, like Watteau, could enjoy the poetry of the *fête
galante*, but, like Watteau, he could also 'understand and
despise it', and then he uses it ironically in a way that fore-
shadows the art of Congreve and Pope:

> Think what a wretched thing is she,
>   Whose Stars contrive, in spight,
> The Morning of her love should be
>   Her fading Beauties Night.
>
> Then if, to make your ruine more,
>   You'll peevishly be coy,
> Dye with the Scandal of a Whore,
>   And never know the Joy.

Another ironic song is more brutal. It is a sort of parody of
'heroic' subject matter which reminds the reader of the bitter
anti-romanticism of the twentieth century:

> The utmost Grace the *Greeks* could shew,
>   When to the *Trojans* they grew kind,
> Was with their Arms to let 'em go,
>   And leave their lingring wives behind.
> They beat the Men, and burnt the Town,
> Then all the Baggage was their own.

Rochester's best songs, however, like the best of Sedley's, are
the 'language of the heart', but they have a music and a
crystalline beauty of phrase which Sedley rarely achieved.
The combination of perfection of form with intensity of
passion in three or four of these little poems can be paralleled
only in the best work of Catullus, Burns and Heine.

   At moments like these he found the 'felicity & glory' of
which he had written to Lady Rochester. In *Love and Life*,
one of his greatest lyrics, he imagines that such moments of

ecstasy might be enjoyed without reference to the follies and
impertinences of daily life:

> All my past Life is mine no more,
>   The flying hours are gone:
> Like transitory Dreams giv'n o're,
> Whose Images are kept in store,
>   By Memory alone.
>
> The Time that is to come is not,
>   How can it then be mine?
> The present Moment's all my lot; . . .

But the dream of *Love and Life* could be fulfilled only at rare
moments. The world as revealed in the hard light of the new
philosophy and already vulgarised by the domination of
money power was an ugly spectacle. Rochester's superiority
to the other wits lies chiefly in the fact that he not only perceived this ugliness but used it as the material for poetry. His
most impressive and memorable writing is to be found in his
realistic and satiric poems. Like Swift, he is a great satirist
because he has a drama in his soul. He has an artist's delight
in the variety and movement of Restoration England, and in
poems like *A Letter from Artemisa*, *Timon* and *Tunbridge
Wells* he sketches the pageant with the power and gusto of
a Hogaith. Yet with another side of his mind he sees it all
as a 'universe of death' full of stupidity, affectation and
cowardly betrayals. It is the clash between his moral idealism
and his clear-sighted perception of the condition of contemporary humanity that produces some of his finest satiric
work, such as the mordant sketch of the harlot Corinna (see
below, p. 198). The object of poetry like this is not to induce
a dreamlike condition in the reader but to bring him close to
actuality and make him feel its ugliness and absurdity and
also its pathos and grandeur. There is none of what Hobbes

calls 'the frequencie of insignificant speech' in Rochester's satires. Every word has the weight of passion behind its conscious, rational meaning. The forms that appeal to him particularly are the dramatic dialogue and monologue, and his ability as an actor serves him here as it served him in his exploits at Whitehall and on Tower Hill. His *Maim'd Debauchee* is a dramatic monologue that Browning never excelled. This poem was described by Charles Whibley as 'a masterpiece of heroic irony'. 'You can but say of it', writes that admirable critic, 'that it bears the stamp of Rochester's vigour and sincerity in every line.'

His great philosophic poems are the lines *Upon Nothing*, the poem on Death adapted from Seneca, the *Satyr upon Mankind* and *Consideratus Considerandus*.[1] The poem *Upon Nothing*, written in a metre suggested by the old religious poet Quarles, was possibly inspired by a passage in *Leviathan* where Hobbes calls all names except those that signify bodies, sense impressions, parts of speech or relations between words 'insignificant sounds' or 'names of nothing'. Rochester in a flash of vision sees Nothing as the oldest of all powers, a venerable anarch like Milton's Chaos and the fountain-head of all the mummeries of religion and statecraft. This is the last great metaphysical poem of the seventeenth century, rivalling the best work of Donne in its fusion of subtle thought, imagination and irony. The poem on Death is a greater work than the fine Latin lyric which inspired it. It is no mere translation but an original poem based on hints from Seneca. Lucretius, who was one of Rochester's favourite writers, has counted for something here as well as Seneca, and the poem has a quality resembling the famous lines on Death in the third book of the *De Natura Rerum*. Rochester's mind, like that of Lucretius, is essentially religious and his poem is really a hymn to the grandeur of

[1] See below, pp. 209, 210.

death and a repudiation of the superstitions which have obscured it. The *Satyr Against Mankind* is Rochester's most ambitious performance. It is the poetry of argument indeed, but its passionate vehemence is different from the cool reasoning of Dryden and Pope. It is the most courageous expression in English of the moral crisis of the Western world in the later seventeenth century, when the new philosophies of Descartes, Hobbes and Spinoza had shattered the old unified world picture of the religious tradition, and man was seen for the first time as an individual, miserable and insignificant in a hostile or indifferent universe. The place of Rochester's poem is beside the great things in Swift, and it recalls the king of Brobdingnag's denunciation of the human race. There is nothing like it in English poetry until the First World War produced a similar moral indignation in the work of Wilfred Owen.

Rochester was rightly described by Voltaire as 'grand poète et homme de génie'. Like Marlowe before him and Byron after him, he is one of those dynamic spirits who disturb the complacency of their contemporaries by their intellectual daring and the terrible clarity of their vision.

Several of Rochester's poems were published during his lifetime as broadsides, but the first collection in book form did not appear till soon after his death in 1680. This was a badly printed little book professing on its title page to contain *Poems on Several Occasions. By the Right Honourable, the E. of R.*, and to have been printed at Antwerp. It includes some of Rochester's best known works, together with a number of poems which are certainly by other authors. An enlarged form of this edition, including more spurious poems as well as others which are genuine, was published by Andrew Thorncome in 1685. In the same year a quarto edition of Rochester's tragedy *Valentinian*, adapted from Fletcher's play of the same name, was published with an interesting preface by his friend Robert Wolseley. In 1691 the well known publisher Jacob Tonson produced a collection of Rochester's works edited by Thomas Rymer. It includes sixteen genuine poems which had appeared in previous editions, as well as twenty-three others, which are probably all authentic, *Valentinian* and *Alexander Bendo's Advertisement*. It does not, however, profess to be a complete edition. Tonson's edition was reprinted in 1696, 1705 and, with important additions, in 1714. Other poems by Rochester appeared in various collections and a great deal of spurious material (mostly pornographic) was fathered on him in editions which appeared during the eighteenth century.

Except where another source is indicated, the text of the poems in the following selection is that of Tonson's edition of 1691. I have given the *Satyr against Mankind* in the text of 1680 as this includes the 'Postscript' (ll. 174–224) which does not appear in the edition of 1691. Two fine lyrics are printed from the unique MS. in Rochester's autograph in the Duke of Portland's collection now in the Library of the University of Nottingham (referred to as 'Portland MS.'), a song from *Valentinian* is taken from the quarto of 1685 and two poems probably written by Rochester on his deathbed from Thorncome's edition of 1685, where they appear to have been printed for the first time.

Poems by John Wilmot, Earl of Rochester

A SONG

Absent from thee I languish still,
 Then ask me not, when I return?
The straying Fool 'twill plainly kill,
 To wish all Day, all Night to Mourn.

Dear; from thine Arms then let me flie,
 That my fantastick Mind may prove
The Torments it deserves to try,
 That tears my fixt Heart from my Love.

When wearied with a world of Woe
 To thy safe Bosom I retire,
Where Love, and Peace, and Truth does flow,
 May I contented there expire.

Lest once more wand'ring from that Heav'n,
 I fall on some base heart unblest;
Faithless to thee, False, unforgiv'n,
 And lose my Everlasting Rest.

THE MISTRESS: A SONG

An Age in her Embraces past,
  Would seem a Winters day;
Where Life and Light, with envious hast,
  Are torn and snatch'd away.

But, oh! how slowly Minutes rowl,
  When absent from her Eyes;
That feed my Love, which is my Soul,
  It languishes and dyes.

For then no more a Soul but shade,
  It mournfully does move;
And haunts my Breast, by absence made
  The living Tomb of Love.

You Wiser men despise me not;
  Whose Love-sick Fancy raves,
On Shades of Souls, and Heaven knows what;
  Short Ages live in Graves.

When e're those wounding Eyes, so full
  Of Sweetness, you did see;
Had you not been profoundly dull,
  You had gone mad like me.

Nor Censure us, You who perceive
  My best belov'd and me,
Sigh and lament, Complain and grive,
  You think we disagree.

Alas! 'tis Sacred Jealousie,
  Love rais'd to an Extream;
The only Proof 'twixt her and me,
  We love, and do not dream.

Fantastick Fancies fondly move;
   And in frail Joys believe:
Taking false Pleasure for true Love;
   But Pain can ne're deceive.

Kind Jealous Doubts, tormenting Fears.
   And Anxious Cares, when past;
Prove our Hearts Treasure fixt and dear,
   And make us blest at last.

GRECIAN KINDNESS: A SONG

The utmost Grace the *Greeks* could shew,
   When to the *Trojans* they grew kind,
Was with their Arms to let 'em go,
   And leave their lingring Wives behind.
They beat the Men, and burnt the Town,
Then all the Baggage was their own.

There the kind Deity of Wine
   Kiss'd the soft wanton God of Love;
This clapp'd his Wings, that press'd his Vine;
   And their best Pow'rs united move.
While each brave *Greek* embrac'd his Punk,
Lull'd her asleep, and then grew drunk.

A SONG

Phillis, be gentler, I advise;
    Make up for time mispent,
When Beauty on its Death-bed lyes,
    'Tis high time to repent.

Such is the Malice of your Fate,
    That makes you old so soon;
Your pleasure ever comes too late,
    How early e're begun.

Think what a wretched thing is she,
    Whose Stars contrive, in spight,
The Morning of her love should be
    Her fading Beauties Night.

Then if, to make your ruine more,
    You'll peevishly be coy,
Dye with the Scandal of a Whore,
    And never know the Joy

LOVE AND LIFE: A SONG

All my past Life is mine no more,
   The flying hours are gone:
Like transitory Dreams giv'n o're,
Whose Images are kept in store
   By Memory alone.

The Time that is to come is not;
   How can it then be mine?
The present Moment's all my lot;
And that, as fast as it is got,
   Phillis, is only thine.

Then talk not of Inconstancy,
   False Hearts, and broken Vows;
If I, by Miracle, can be
This live-long Minute true to thee,
   'Tis all that Heav'n allows.

A SONG

My dear Mistress has a Heart
   Soft as those kind looks she gave me;
When with Love's resistless Art,
   And her Eyes she did enslave me.
But her Constancy's so weak,
   She's so wild, and apt to wander;
That my jealous Heart wou'd break,
   Should we live one day asunder.

Melting Joys about her move,
   Killing Pleasures, wounding Blisses;
She can dress her Eyes in Love,
   And her Lips can arm with Kisses.
Angels listen when she speaks,
   She's my delight, all Mankinds wonder:
But my jealous Heart would break,
   Should we live one day asunder.

A SONG

While on those lovely looks I gaze,
   To see a Wretch persuing,
In Raptures of a blest amaze,
   His pleasing happy Ruine:
'Tis not for pity that I move;
   His Fate is too aspiring,
Whose Heart, broke with a load of Love,
   Dies wishing and admiring.

But if this Murder you'd forego,
   Your Slave from Death removing;
Let me your Art of Charming know,
   Or learn you mine of Loving.
But whether Life, or Death, betide,
   In love 'tis equal Measure,
The Victor lives with empty Pride;
   The Vanquish'd die with Pleasure.

A SONG

Nymph Injurious Charmer of my vanquisht Heart,
   Canst thou feel Love, and yet no pity know?
  Since of my self from thee I cannot part,
   Invent some gentle Way to let me go.
    For what with Joy thou didst obtain,
     And I with more did give;
    In time will make thee false and vain,
     And me unfit to live.

Shepherd Frail Angel, that wou'dst leave a Heart forlorn,
   With vain pretence falshood therein might lye;
  Seek not to cast wild shadows o're your scorn,
   You cannot sooner change than I can dye.
    To tedious life I'le never fall,
     Thrown from thy dear lov'd Breast;
    He merits not to live at all,
     Who cares to live unblest.

Chorus Then let our flaming Hearts be joyn'd;
   While in that sacred fire;
  E'er thou prove false, or I unkind,
   Together both expire.

From *Valentinian, A Tragedy As 'tis alter'd by the*
Late Earl of Rochester, 4to, 1685

UPON DRINKING IN A BOWL

Vulcan contrive me such a Cup,
    As *Nestor* us'd of old.
Shew all thy Skill to trim it up,
    Damask it round with Gold.

Make it so large, that, fill'd with Sack,
    Up to the swelling Brim;
Vast Toasts, on the delicious Lake,
    Like Ships at Sea, may swim.

Engrave not Battel on his Cheek,
    With War I've nought to do:
I'm none of those that took *Mastrick*,*
    Nor *Yarmouth* Leaguer* knew.

Let it no name of Planets tell,
    Fixt Stars, or Constellations;
For I am no Sir *Sindrophel*,*
    Nor none of his Relations.

But carve thereon a spreading Vine;
    Then add two lovely Boys;
Their Limbs in amorous Folds intwine
    The Type of future Joys.

Cupid and *Bacchus* my Saints are,
    May Drink and Love still reign:
With Wine I wash away my Cares,
    And then to Love again.

This poem is a free adaptation or 'imitation' of the eighteenth ode of Anacreon.
11 *Mastrick:* Maastricht, the Dutch fortress taken by the French with English help on 1 July 1673. Rochester may also be alluding to a mimic siege of Maastricht staged at Windsor for the Court in the summer of 1674.
12 *Yarmouth Leaguer:* 'leaguer' meant a military camp. This refers to a troop concentration at Yarmouth for a projected invasion of Holland in July 1673.
15 *Sir Sindrophel:* probably Sidrophil, the comic astronomer in *Hudibras*.

A SONG

'Twas a dispute 'twixt heav'n and Earth
    Which had produc't the Nobler birth:
For Heav'n, Appear'd Cynthya with all her Trayne,
      Till you came forth
    More glorious and more Worth,
Than shee with all those trembling imps of Light
      With which This Envious Queene of night
Had Proudly deck't her Conquer'd self in Vaine.

I must have perrisht in that first surprize
      Had I beheld your Eyes.
Love, like Appollo when he would inspire
Some holy brest, laid all his gloryes by.
      Els the God cloath'd in his heavnly fire
    Would have possest too powerfully,
And making of his Preist A sacrifice
Had so return'd unhallow'd to the Skyes.

Portland MS

SONG

Leave this gawdy guilded Stage
From custome more than use frequented;
Where fooles of either sex and age
Crowd to see themselves presented.
To loves Theatre the Bed
Youth and beauty fly together
And Act soe well it may be said
The Lawrell there was due to either:
Twixt strifes of Love and war the difference Lies in this
When neither overcomes Loves triumph greater is.

Portland MS

Both in this and the preceding poem the exact spelling of Rochester's autograph is retained.

THE MAIM'D DEBAUCHEE

As some brave *Admiral* in former War
  Depriv'd of Force, but prest with Courage still,
Two Rival Fleets appearing from afar,
  Crawls to the top of an adjacent Hill.

From whence (with thoughts full of concern) he views
  The Wise, and daring, Conduct of the Fight:
And each bold Action to his mind renews;
  His present Glory, and his past Delight.

From his fierce Eyes flashes of Rage he throws,
  As from black Clouds when Lightning breaks away,
Transported thinks himself among his Foes,
  And absent, yet enjoys the bloody Day.

So when my days of Impotence approach,
  And I'me by Love and Wines unlucky Chance,
Driv'n from the pleasing Billows of Debauch,
  On the dull Shore of lazy Temperance.

My pains at last some respite shall afford,
  While I behold the Battels you maintain:
When Fleets of Glasses sail around the Board,
  From whose Broad-Sides Volleys of Wit shall rain.

Nor shall the sight of Honourable Scars,
  Which my too forward Valour did procure,
Frighten new listed Souldiers from the Wars,
  Past Joys have more than paid what I endure.

Shou'd some brave Youth (worth being drunk) prove nice,
  And from his fair inviter meanly shrink,
'Twould please the Ghost of my departed Vice,
  If, at my Counsel, He repent and drink.

Or shou'd some cold complexion'd Sot forbid,
   With his dull Morals, our Nights brisk Alarms;
I'le fire his Blood, by telling what I did,
   When I was strong, and able to bear Arms.

I'le tell of Whores attacqu'd their Lords at home,
   Bawds Quarters beaten up, and Fortress won:
Windows demolish'd, Watches overcome,
   And handsome ills by my contrivance done.

With Tales like these I will such heat inspire,
   As to important mischief shall incline:
I'le make 'em long some Ancient Church to fire,
   And fear no lewdness they're call'd to by Wine.

Thus States-men like I'le saucily impose,
   And, safe from danger, valiantly advise:
Shelter'd in impotence urge you to blows,
   And, being good for nothing else, be wise.

UPON NOTHING

Nothing, thou Elder Brother ev'n to Shade,
Thou hadst a being e're the World was made
And (well fixt) art alone, of ending not afraid.

E're time and place were, time and place were not,
When Primitive *Nothing* something strait begot,
Then all proceeded from the great united—What.

Something the Gen'ral Attribute of all,
Sever'd from thee, it's sole Original,
Into thy boundless self must undistinguish'd fall.

Yet something did thy mighty Pow'r command,
And from thy fruitful emptiness's hand,
Snatch'd Men, Beasts, Birds, Fire, Air, and Land.

Matter, the wicked'st off-spring of thy Race,
By Form assisted flew from thy Embrace,
And Rebel Light obscur'd thy reverend dusky Face.

With Form, and Matter, time and place did joyn,
Body, thy Foe, with thee did Leagues combine,
To spoil thy peaceful Realm, and ruine all thy Line.

But turn-Coat Time assists the Foe in vain,
And brib'd by thee, assists thy short-liv'd Reign,
And to thy hungry Womb, drives back thy Slaves again.

Tho' Mysteries are barr'd from Laick Eyes,
And the Divine alone, with Warrant, pryes
Into thy Bosom, where the truth in private lies.

Yet this of thee the wise may freely say,
Thou from the virtuous nothing tak'st away,
And to be part with thee the Wicked wisely pray.

Great Negative, how vainly wou'd the Wise
Enquire, define, distinguish, teach, devise?
Didst thou not stand to point their dull Philosophies.

Is, or *is not*, the two great Ends of Fate,
And, true, or false, the subject of debate,
That perfect, or destroy, the vast designs of Fate,

When they have rack'd the *Politician's* Breast,
Within thy Bosom most securely rest,
And, when reduc'd to thee, are least unsafe and best.

But, *Nothing*, why does *Something* still permit,
That Sacred Monarchs should at Council sit,
With Persons highly thought at best for nothing fit.

Whilst weighty *Something* modestly abstains,
From Princes Coffers, and from States-Mens Brains,
And nothing there like stately *Nothing* reigns.

Nothing who dwell'st with Fools in grave Disguise,
For whom they Reverend Shapes, and Forms devise,
Lawn Sleeves, and Furs, and Gowns, when they like thee
     look wise.

French Truth, *Dutch* Prowess, *Brittish* Policy,
Hibernian Learning; *Scotch* Civility,
Spaniards Dispatch, *Danes* Wit, are mainly seen in thee.

The great Man's Gratitude to his best Friend,
Kings Promises, Whores Vows, tow'rd thee they bend,
Flow swiftly into thee, and in thee ever end.

CORINNA

The meanest, common Slut, who long has grown
The jeast and scorn, of ev'ry Pit Buffoon;
Had yet left Charms enough to have subdu'd
Some Fop or other; fond to be thought lewd.
*Foster** could make an *Irish* Lord a *Nokes*;*
And *Betty Morris** had her City Cokes.*
A Woman's ne're so ruin'd, but she can
Be still reveng'd on her undoer, Man:
How lost soe're She'l find some Lover more,
A more abandon'd Fool than she a Whore.
That wretched thing *Corinna*, who has run
Through all the sev'ral ways of being undone:
Cozen'd at first by Love, and living then
By turning to the too-dear-bought cheat on Men:
Gay were the hours, and wing'd with joy they flew,
When first the Town her early Beauties knew:
Courted, admir'd, and lov'd, with Presents fed;
Youth in her Looks, and Pleasure in her Bed:
'Till Fate, or her ill Angel, thought it fit
To make her doat upon a man of Wit:
Who found 'twas dull to love above a day;
Made his ill-natur'd jeast, and went away.
Now scorn'd of all, forsaken, and opprest,
She's a *Memento Mori* to the rest:
Diseas'd, decay'd, to take up half a Crown
Must mortgage her Long Scarf, and Manto Gown;

These lines are an extract from Rochester's satire *A Letter from Artemisa in the Town to Cloe in the Country*. They are placed in the mouth of a country lady who is explaining to Artemisa that fools are preferable to wits as lovers.
5 *Foster:* this is possibly Mrs Foster a friend of the actress Mrs Knipp, mentioned several times by Pepys in his Diary. *Nokes:* a ninny or fool.
6 *Betty Morris:* apparently a woman of the Town; nothing seems to be known about her. *Cokes:* an obsolete word for a silly fellow, possibly related to 'Cockney'.

Poor Creature, who unheard of, as a Flie,
In some dark hole must all the Winter lye;
And want and dirt, endure a whole half year,
That, for one month, she Tawdry may appear.
In *Easter* Term she gets her a new Gown;
When my young Master's Worship comes to Town....

A SATYR AGAINST MANKIND

Were I (who to my cost already am
One of those strange prodigious Creatures *Man*.)
A Spirit free, to choose for my own share,
What case of Flesh, and Blood I pleas'd to weare,
I'd be a *Dog*, a *Monkey*, or a *Bear*,
Or any thing, but that vain *Animal*,
Who is so proud of being rational.
The senses are too gross; and he'll contrive
A Sixth, to contradict the other Five;
And before certain instinct, will preferr
Reason, which Fifty times for one does err.
Reason, an *Ignis fatuus*, in the *Mind*,
Which leaving light of Nature, sense, behind;
Pathless, and dang'rous wandring ways it takes,
Through errors, Fenny-*Boggs*, and Thorny *Brakes*:
Whilst the misguided follower, climbs with pain,
Mountains of Whimsies, heapt in his own *Brain*;
Stumbling from thought to thought, falls head-long down,
Into doubt's boundless Sea, where like to drown
Books bear him up a while, and make him try
To swim with Bladders of *Philosophy*:
In hopes still t'oretake th'escaping light,
The *Vapour* dances in his dazled Sight,
'Till spent, it leaves him to eternal Night.
Then Old Age, and experience, hand in hand,
Lead him to death, and make him understand,
After a search so painful, and so long,
That all his Life he has been in the wrong.

This poem is simply headed 'Satyr' in the edition of 1680; the title *A Satyr against Mankind* appears in the broadside edition of 1679 and in Tonson's edition of 1691. The poem was first printed anonymously as a broadside in June 1679, but seems to have been circulating in MS. as early as the spring of 1676. It owes something to the Eighth Satire of Boileau, but probably even more to Montaigne, especially his *Apologie de Raimond Sebond*.

Hudled in Dirt, the reas'ning *Engine* lyes,
Who was so proud, so witty, and so wise:
Pride drew him in, as *Cheats*, their *Bubbles*, catch,
And made him venture, to be made a *Wretch*:
His wisdom did his happiness destroy,
Aiming to know that* World he shou'd enjoy.
And *Wit* was his vain frivolous pretence,
Of pleasing others, at his own expence.
For *Witts* are treated just like common *Whores*;
First they're enjoy'd, and then kickt out of *Doores*:
The pleasure past, a threat'ning doubt remains,
That frights th' enjoyer with succeeding pains.
Women, and *Men* of *Wit*, are dang'rous Tools,
And ever fatal to admiring *Fools*.
Pleasure allures, and when the *Fopps* escape,
'Tis not that they're belov'd, but fortunate,
And therefore what they fear, at heart* they hate.

But now methinks some formal Band, and Beard
Takes me to task; come on Sir I'm prepar'd:
Then by your favour, any thing that's writ
Against this gibing, jingling knack, call'd Wit,
Likes me abundantly, but you take care,
Upon this point, not to be too severe,
Perhaps my Muse *were fitter for this part:*
For I profess, I can be very smart
On Wit, *which I abhor with all my heart:*
I long to lash it, in some sharp Essay,
But your grand indiscretion bids me stay,
And turns my Tide of Ink another way.
What Rage ferments in your degen'rate mind,
To make you rail at Reason, and Mankind?

34 *that:* 1680 reads 'what', 1691 'the'; 'that' is obviously correct.
45 *heart:* 1680 reads 'least', 1691 'heart', obviously the correct reading.

Bless'd glorious Man! *to whom alone kind* Heav'n
An everlasting Soul *has freely giv'n;*
Whom his great Maker *took such care to make,*
That from himself he did the Image *take,*
And this fair Frame in shining Reason *drest,*
To dignifie his Nature, *above Beast,*
Reason, *by whose aspiring influence,*
We take a flight beyond material sense,
Dive into Mysteries, then soaring pierce
The flaming limits of the Universe,
Search Heav'n and Hell, find out what's acted there,
And give the World true grounds of hope and fear.

Hold, mighty Man, I cry; all this we know,
From the Pathetique Pen of *Ingello;*[*]
From *Patrick's Pilgrim, Sibb's soliloquies,*[*]
And 'tis this very reason I despise,
This supernat'ral gift, that makes a *Myte,*
Think he is the Image of the Infinite;
Comparing his short life, void of all rest,
To the *Eternal,* and the ever blest;
This busie, puzling, stirrer up of doubt,
That frames deep *Mysteries,* then finds 'em out;
Filling with Frantick Crowds of thinking *Fools,*
Those rev'rend *Bedlams, Colledges* and *Schools,*
Born on whose Wings, each heavy *Sot* can pierce,
The limits of the boundless Universe:

73 *Ingello:* Nathaniel Ingelo (?1621–83), author of a dreary allegorical romance called *Bentivolio and Urania* (1660).

74 *Patrick's Pilgrim:* only the initial letter of Patrick is given in 1680. The whole name appears in 1691. The reference is to *The Parable of the Pilgrims,* a religious allegory by Simon Patrick, Bishop of Ely, published in 1664.

Sibbs: again only the initial letter appears in 1680, but the complete name in 1691. Richard Sibbes (1577–1635) was a Puritan divine and author of numerous religious works.

Soliloquies: this is the reading of 1691. 1680 has 'replys', obviously a mistake

So charming Oyntments make an old *Witch* flie,
And bear a cripled Carkass through the Skie.
'Tis this exalted Pow'r, whose bus'ness lies,
In *Nonsense*, and impossibilities:
This made a Whimsical *Philosopher*,
Before the spacious *World* his *Tub* prefer:
And we have modern Cloyster'd Coxcombs, who
Retire to think, cause they have naught to do.
But thoughts are giv'n for Actions government;
Where Action ceases, thought's impertinent.
Our *Sphere* of Action is lifes happiness,
And he that thinks Beyond, thinks like an *Ass*.
Thus whilst 'gainst false reas'ning I inveigh,
I own right *Reason*, which I would obey:
That *Reason* that distinguishes by sense,
And gives us *Rules* of good and ill from thence:
That bounds desires, with a reforming Will,
To keep 'em more in vigour, not to kill.
Your *Reason* hinders; mine helps t'enjoy
Renewing Appetites, yours wou'd destroy.
My Reason is my *Friend*, yours is a *Cheat*,
Hunger calls out, my Reason bids me eat;
Perversely yours, your Appetite does mock;
This asks for Food, that answers what's a Clock?

This plain distinction, Sir, your doubt secures;
'Tis not true Reason I despise, but yours.
Thus, I think Reason righted: but for *Man*,
I'le nere recant, defend him if you can.
For all his Pride, and his Philosophy,
'Tis evident, *Beasts* are, in their degree,
As wise at least, and better far than he.
Those *Creatures* are the wisest, who attain,
By surest means, the ends at which they aim.

If therefore *Jowler* finds, and Kills his Hares,
Better than *Meres** supplyes Committee Chairs;
Though one's a *States-man*, th' other but a *Hound*;
Jowler, in Justice, wou'd be wiser found.

You see how far *Man's* wisedom here extends:
Look next, if humane Nature makes amends;
Whose Principles, most gen'rous are and just;
And to whose *Moralls* you wou'd sooner trust.
Be Judge your self, I'le bring it to the test,
Which is the basest *Creature, Man*, or *Beast*:
Birds feed on *Birds, Beasts* on each other prey,
But Savage *Man* alone, does *Man*, betray.
Prest by necessity, they Kill for Food;
Man undoes *Man*, to do himself no good.

With Teeth, and Claws by Nature arm'd, they hunt,
Natures allowances to supply their want:
But *Man*, with smiles, embraces, Friendships, praise,
Unhumanely his Fellows life betrays:
With voluntary pains, works his distress;
Not through necessity, but wantonness.

For hunger, or for Love, they fight or tear,
Whilst wretched *Man* is still in Arms for fear:
For fear he armes, and is of Armes afraid;
From fear to fear, successively betray'd,
Base fear, the source whence his best passions came,
His boasted Honor, and his dear-bought Fame,
The lust of Pow'r, to which he's such a *Slave*,
And for the which alone he dares be brave:
To which his various Projects are design'd,
Which makes him gen'rous, affable, and kind:
For which he takes such pains to be thought wise,

120 *Meres:* the full name is only given in 1691. The reference is to Sir Thomas
Meres or Meeres (1635–1715), M.P. for Lincoln in the parliaments of
Charles II, and Commissioner for the Admiralty.

And screws his actions, in a forc'd disguise:
Leads a most tedious life in Misery,
Under laborious, mean *Hypocrisie*.
Look to the bottom of his vast design,
Wherein *Mans* Wisdom, Pow'r, and Glory joyn;
The good he acts, the ill he does endure,
'Tis all from fear, to make himself secure.
Meerly for safety, after Fame we thirst;
For all Men wou'd be *Cowards* if they durst,
And honesty's against all common sense,
Men must be *Knaves*, 'tis in their own defence,
Mankind's dishonest; if you think it fair,
Amongst known *Cheats*, to play upon the square,
You'll be undone...
Nor can weak truth your reputation save;
The *Knaves* will all agree to call you *Knave*.
Wrong'd shall he live, insulted o're, opprest,
Who dares be less a *Villain* than the rest.
Thus Sir you see what humane Nature craves,
Most Men are *Cowards*, all Men shou'd be *Knaves*.
The diff'rence lyes (as far as I can see)
Not in the thing it self, but the degree;
And all the subject Matter of debate,
Is only who's a *Knave* of the first *Rate*.*

[POSTSCRIPT]

All this with indignation have I hurl'd,
At the pretending part of the proud World,
Who swolne with selfish vanity, devise,
False freedomes, holy Cheats, and formal Lyes,

173 ...a *Knave* of the first *Rate:* the shorter version of the poem, as it appears in the broadside of 1679 and Tonson's edition of 1691 stops at this point. In the 1680 text the remaining fifty lines follow without a break but in Tonson's edition of 1714 they are headed 'Postscript'.

Over their fellow *Slaves* to tyrannize.
But if in *Court*, so just a Man there be,
(In *Court*, a just Man, yet unknown to me.)
Who does his needful flattery direct,
Not to oppress, and ruine, but protect;
Since flattery, which way so ever laid,
Is still a Tax on that unhappy Trade.
If so upright a *States-Man*, you can find,
Whose passions bend to his unbyass'd Mind;
Who does his Arts, and *Policies* apply,
To raise his *Country*, not his *Family*;
Nor while his Pride, own'd Avarice withstands,
Receives Aureal Bribes, from Friends corrupted hands.*

Is there a *Church-Man* who on *God* relyes?
Whose Life, his Faith, and Doctrine Justifies?
Not one blown up with vain Prelatique Pride,
Who for reproof of Sins, does *Man* deride:
Whose envious heart with his obstrep'rous sawcy Eloquence,*
Dares chide at *Kings*, and raile at Men of sense.
Who from his Pulpit, vents more peevish Lyes,
More bitter railings, scandals, Calumnies,
Than at a Gossipping, are thrown about,
When the good *Wives* get drunk, and then fall out.
None of that sensuall *Tribe*, whose Tallents lye,
In Avarice, *Pride*, *Sloth*, and *Gluttony*,
Who hunt good Livings, but abhor good Lives,
Whose Lust exalted, to that height arrives,
They act *Adultery* with their own *Wives*.
And e're a score of Years compleated be,
Can from the lofty *Pulpit* proudly see,
Half a Large *Parish*, their own *Progeny*.

189, 190 *Nor while his Pride...corrupted hands* and 195 *Whose envious heart...Eloquence:* the text of these lines is almost certainly corrupt.

Nor doating B——* who wou'd be ador'd,
For domineering at the *Councel Board*;
A greater Fop in business at Fourscore,
Fonder of serious *Toyes*, affected more,
Than the gay glitt'ring *Fool* at Twenty proves,
With all his noise, his tawdrey Clothes, and Loves.
But a meek humble Man, of modest sense,
Who Preaching peace, does practice continence;
Whose pious life's a proof he does believe,
Misterious truths which no *Man* can conceive.
If upon *Earth* there dwell such *God-like Men*,
I'le here recant my *Paradox* to them.
Adore those *Shrines* of *Virtue*, *Homage* pay,
And with the *Rabble World*, their *Laws* obey.
If such there are, yet grant me this at least,
Man differs more from *Man*, than *Man* from *Beast*.

209 *B*——: only the initial appears in the 1680 text and a blank in 1714 in
this place. The reference may be to Thomas Barlow, bishop of Lincoln
(1607–91), a kind of Vicar of Bray, who was one of the first to declare his
loyalty to James II but promptly turned Whig on the accession of William
and Mary.

THE LATTER END OF
THE CHORUS OF THE SECOND ACT OF
SENECA'S TROAS TRANSLATED

After Death nothing is, and nothing Death:
The utmost Limits of a gasp of Breath.
Let the ambitious Zealot lay aside
His hopes of Heav'n; (whose Faith is but his Pride)
Let slavish Souls lay by their Fear,
Nor be concern'd which way, or where,
After this life they shall be hurl'd:
Dead, we become the Lumber of the World;
And to that Mass of Matter shall be swept,
Where things destroy'd, with things unborn are kept;
Devouring time swallows us whole,
Impartial Death confounds Body and Soul.
For Hell, and the foul Fiend that rules
The everlasting fiery Gaols,
Devis'd by Rogues, dreaded by Fools,
With his grim griesly Dog that keeps the Door,
Are senseless Stories, idle Tales,
Dreams, Whimseys, and no more.

This poem is a free adaptation of ll. 397–408 of the *Troades* of Seneca.
Charles Blount wrote to thank Rochester for a copy of this poem in February
1679/80.

PLAIN DEALINGS DOWNFALL

Long time plain dealing in the Hauty Town,
Wandring about, though in thread-bare Gown,
At last unanimously was cry'd down.

When almost starv'd, she to the Countrey fled,
In hopes, though meanly she shou'd there be fed,
And tumble Nightly on a Pea-straw Bed.

But Knav'ry knowing her intent, took post,
And Rumour'd her approach through every Coast,
Vowing his Ruin that shou'd be her host.

Frighted at this, each *Rustick* shut his door,
Bid her be gone, and trouble him no more,
For he that entertain'd her must be poor.

At this grief seiz'd her, grief too great to tell,
When weeping, sighing, fainting, down she fell,
Whil's Knavery Laughing, Rung her passing Bell.

Poems on Several Occasions. Written by a Late Person of
Honour, London, Printed for A. Thorncome, 1685

CONSIDERATUS CONSIDERANDUS

What pleasures can the gaudy World afford?
What true delights do's teeming Nature hoard?
In her great Store-house, where she lays her treasure?
Alas, 'tis all the shaddow of a pleasure;
No true Content in all her works is found,
No sollid Joys in all Earth's spacious round:
For Labouring Man who toils himself in vain,
Eagerly grasping, what creates his pain.
How false and feeble, nay scarce worth a Name,
Are Riches, Honour, Pow'r and babling Fame.
Yet, 'tis for these Men wade through Seas of Blood,
And bold in *Mischief*, Storm to be withstood:
Which when obtained, breed but Stupendious Fear,
Strife, Jelousies, and sleep disturbing care,
No beam of comfort, not a Ray of light
Shines thence to guide us through Fate's Gloomy Night;
But lost in devious Darkness, there we stay,
Bereft of Reason in an endless way;
Vertue's the Sollid good, if any be;
'Tis that Creates our true Felicitie;
Though we Despise, Contemn, and cast it by,
As worthless, or our fatal'st Enemy;
Because our darling lusts it dare controule,
And bound the Roveings of the Madding Soul.
Therefore in garments poor, it still appears,
And sometimes (naked) it no Garment wears;
Shun'd by the Great, and worthless thought by most,
Urg'd to be gone, or wish'd for ever lost;
Yet is it loath to leave our wretched Coast.
But in disguise do's here and there intrude,
Striving to conquer base Ingratitude:
And boldly ventures now and then to Shine,

So to make known it is of Birth divine;
But Clouded oft, it like the Lightning plays,
Loosing as soon as seen it's pointed Rays.
Which Scarceness makes those that are weak in wit,
For Virtue's self, admire it's counterfeit:
With which dam'd *Hippocrites* the World delude,
As we on *Indian Glass*, for Gems intrude.

Poems on Several Occasions

John Sheffield, Duke of
Buckinghamshire

Next them a train of Loyal Peers ascend:
Sharp-judging Adriel, *the Muses Friend,*
Himself a Muse:—in Sanhedrin's debate,
True to his Prince; but not a Slave of State.

DRYDEN, Absalom and Achitophel, Part I

John Sheffield
Duke of Buckinghamshire
1648-1721

ACCORDING TO Anthony à Wood, the guests who used to attend the suppers of Charles II in the apartments of the duchess of Portsmouth, William Chiffinch and Nell Gwyn in 1676 and 1677 included Thomas Killigrew, Henry Savile, Henry Guy, Baptist May, and the earls of Dorset, Rochester and Mulgrave. John Sheffield, earl of Mulgrave, the last-named of these favourite companions of the king, was a tall, ungainly man with a narrow chest and shoulders, a harsh voice and a loud laugh. He is the least interesting and attractive character among the famous group of wits, but he is by no means without merit as a writer of prose and verse, and he certainly deserves a place in a representative selection of the literary courtiers of the Restoration.

The Sheffields were an ancient and distinguished Lincolnshire family. The founder of their fortunes was a Sir Robert Sheffield of Butterwick, who was Recorder of London and Speaker of the Commons in the reign of Henry VIII. His grandson, Edmund, was created Baron Sheffield in 1547. This Lord Sheffield led a force to suppress Ket's Rebellion and was killed in the fighting at Norwich in 1549. He was a musician and poet, and wrote 'a book of sonnetts according to the Italian fashion', which has not survived. He had a grandson also called Edmund, who inherited the title, and had a distinguished career as a naval officer in the reign of Elizabeth. He commanded a ship called *The White Bear* in the battle against the Spanish Armada and was knighted by Lord Howard of Effingham. Elizabeth granted him the manor of Mulgrave in Yorkshire in 1591. He was lord lieutenant of Yorkshire and president of the Council of the North under James I, and he was created earl of Mulgrave at the coronation of Charles I. In spite of this mark of royal favour, he joined the opposition to the court in his old age and supported the Parliament in the Civil War. He died at the age of eighty-two in 1646. He married twice, and had six sons, all of whom predeceased him. Three were drowned in the Humber and their death was lamented in an elegy by Michael Drayton.

The title and estates descended to the grandson of the first Earl of Mulgrave, who became a member of Cromwell's Council, and was one of the peers summoned by the Protector to his Upper House. He married Lady Elizabeth Cranfield, daughter of Lionel Cranfield, earl of Middlesex, and sister of the Lady Frances Cranfield, who married Richard Sackville, Lord Buckhurst, afterwards fifth earl of Dorset.[1] They had one son, John, born in 1649, who was thus the first cousin of Charles Sackville, earl of Dorset, the poet. On the death of his father in 1658, John Sheffield became third earl of Mulgrave when he was nine years old.

The widow of the second earl married again, and left the education of her son to a 'governor' or tutor, who is said to have been a learned man but to have 'too much neglected the studies of his Pupil'. When they were travelling in France, he solemnly warned the young earl against kneeling when the Host was carried in procession in the streets, 'representing it as an act of direct idolatry which a Protestant ought to suffer death itself rather than commit'. In those days it was dangerous in Catholic countries to refuse to kneel when the consecrated elements were carried through the streets. One day the tutor and his pupil met a procession with the Host,

[1] See below, p. 112.

and the young peer dutifully turned aside into a shop to avoid it. As he did so he tumbled over the tutor, who had fallen on his knees as soon as he saw the procession approaching. After that the tutor's authority over his pupil was considerably diminished. Mulgrave, like Rochester, seems to have been travelling on the Continent in the years immediately following the Restoration, and he probably appeared at court in 1665, when he was seventeen. He was apparently accepted as a member of the 'merry gang' at that time, and, like Rochester, Etherege and Savile, he belonged to the fast set called the Ballers. Like the others, he adopted the fashionable philosophy of Hobbes, which seemed, in his words, 'plain Reason's Light', putting 'fantastick Forms to shamefull Flight'.[1] The anonymous 'character' of Sheffield published in 1729 gives some information about this part of his career, which, if it is true, is very creditable to him, and is a remarkable proof of the respect in which learning was held by the Restoration courtiers. He found, we are told, 'upon conversing with the greatest genius's of the Age that he had not been fully instructed in many parts of literature; and resolved to begin then to inform himself in what he perceiv'd he was deficient. In order to do this the better, he shut himself up several hours a day from his pleasures and his friends; and by some years application in that manner, improv'd himself to the degree of learning he arrived at.' His short commentary on some of Cicero's letters, his translation of the Letter from Epicurus to Menoecus, and his account of Herod and Mark Antony, all printed in his collected works, show that he was genuinely interested in classical learning and had read fairly widely in ancient literature.

In 1666, fired by the example of the young earl of Ossory, Mulgrave went as a volunteer to the fleet, and served for six weeks with Lord Blany, Sir Thomas Clifford and Henry

[1] See below, p. 242.

Savile in the flagship of Prince Rupert and the duke of
Albemarle. When the Dutch Fleet under De Ruyter attacked
Chatham, the command of one of the troops of horse raised
to repel the threatened invasion was given to Mulgrave on
13 June 1667, and he was 'so foolishly fond of it that he was
as sorry for being disbanded at the Peace as though he had
been a meer soldier of Fortune'. There is no further record
of his activities till November, 1669, when he quarrelled with
Rochester and challenged him to a duel.[1] At this time he
appears to have quarrelled with all the wits except Etherege,
with whom he was still on good terms in the reign of James II.
Their opinion of him is probably represented by some lines
ascribed to Rochester, where he is satirised under the name
of *My Lord All Pride*, and his ungainly figure compared to
that of an elephant at a fair:

> So have I seen at *Smithfields* wondrous *Fair*,
> When all his *Brother Monsters* florish there;
> A *Lubbard Elephant*, divert the *Town*,
> With making *Legs*, and shooting off a *Gun*.

Mulgrave was serving with the fleet again against the Dutch
in 1673. At first he 'waited on the duke of York' in his own
ship, but later transferred to the *Victory*, commanded by his
friend and kinsman the earl of Ossory. He took part in the
battle of Southwold Bay, where he behaved himself with
such distinction that he was congratulated by the king and
was given command of the *Royal Katherine*, the best second-
rate ship in the Navy, which had been taken by the Dutch
and recaptured by a handful of English sailors under a
Puritan boatswain called Small. The earl of Mulgrave took
a liking to this man, and the alliance between the haughty
aristocrat and the 'sober, meek and quiet' nonconformist

[1] An account of this strange encounter between the solemn, rather owlish
Mulgrave and his ironic and humorous opponent will be found on pp. 157,
158.

'who seemed rather a shepherd than a soldier and was a heroe in the shape of a Saint' is one of the curiosities of seventeenth-century friendship. At this time Mulgrave was high in the favour of Charles II. In February 1673, he was appointed a gentleman of the bedchamber; in December of the same year he became colonel of the Old Holland Regiment of Foot, and on 23 April 1674, he was admitted to the Order of the Garter. Shortly afterwards, we are told, he served in a campaign under Turenne.

Mulgrave's close association with Dryden is marked by the dedication to him by the Laureate in 1676 of *Aurengzebe*, the last and best of Dryden's rhyming heroic plays. In his Epistle Dedicatory to this play Dryden praises Mulgrave for his 'contempt of popular applause' and his 'retired virtue'. We learn also from this dedication that Mulgrave had interested himself in Dryden's scheme for writing an English national epic and had given him an opportunity of 'discoursing it to his Majesty and his royal highness'. In his dedication Dryden delicately hints that the time has come for his noble patron to 'stir up that remembrance in his Majesty', doubtless with a view to obtaining financial assistance to enable him to carry out his grandiose plan. Dryden paid dearly for his alliance with Mulgrave.[1] In 1675 the earl had composed a lampoon, probably as a reply to *My Lord All Pride*, in which he made a venomous attack on Rochester and his friends Sedley and Dorset, and also on the royal mistresses Cleveland and Portsmouth. Dryden seems to have helped him to polish it, and the lines were being circulated in November 1679, when Rochester sent a copy of them to Henry Savile. The lampoon is *An Essay on Satyr*, which has already been quoted in previous chapters.[2]

Mulgrave, by his own confession, deliberately fomented

[1] See above, pp. 161-3.
[2] See above, pp. 38, 120, 163.

trouble between the duke of York and his nephew, the duke of Monmouth. After the Old Holland Regiment was disbanded on the conclusion of peace, he coveted the command of the First Regiment of Foot Guards, and the duke of York agreed to obtain permission for him to buy out Colonel Russell, who was commanding it. Monmouth, having quarrelled with Mulgrave, went to the king privately, and obtained the command for himself, agreeing to relinquish his captaincy of the First Troop of the Horse Guards to Lord Ossory. Consequently, when the duke of York suggested Mulgrave as colonel of the First Foot Guards he was told by the king that the post was already disposed of. Mulgrave, in his own words, could not 'lose so fair an occasion to part the two Dukes forever...'. He therefore insinuated to York that Monmouth must have 'some ill design' in wanting to exchange the showy position of captain of the First Troop of Horse Guards for the much less imposing colonelcy of a regiment of Foot Guards. His suggestion was apparently that Monmouth might be in a better position to carry out a successful *coup d'état* if he had twenty-four companies of foot at his disposal than if he had only a single troop of horse. In the end the command went neither to Mulgrave nor to Monmouth, but, when Monmouth was disgraced and stripped of all his offices, Mulgrave was given a fat slice of the spoils in the form of the governorship of Hull and the lord lieutenancy of Yorkshire.

Tangier, the North African port which Catherine of Braganza had brought to Charles II as part of her dowry, was in serious danger of falling into the hands of the Moors in the summer of 1680, and, to reinforce the garrison, it was decided to send a force of one thousand two hundred infantry and three hundred cavalry under the command of Mulgrave, who was to be accompanied by Lords Plymouth, Mordant and Lumley and other aristocratic volunteers. They embarked at Portsmouth on 13 June, and according to Mulgrave's own account, the ship allotted to him was in such a bad state that the captain declared that he was afraid to sail in her. The king 'either from laziness of temper' or 'because he was just then more indifferent than he used to be about my lord's safety', refused to listen to the earl's complaints. Mulgrave, however, in spite of the warnings of his friends, resolved to take the risk, though he advised several volunteers of distinction not to follow his example. The young earl of Plymouth, a natural son of the king, insisted on accompanying him. Fortunately they had fine weather all the way, and, though the ship leaked and had to be constantly pumped, they reached their destination safely. Throughout the voyage Mulgrave refused to have the king's health drunk at his table, saying 'he must first get out of his rotten ship before he could make that health go merrily round'. He amused himself while he was at sea by writing a poem in heroic couplets called *The Vision*, from which it appears that he was violently in love with a married woman who had hitherto repulsed his advances. On 16 June a four months' armistice had been concluded with the Moors, and it does not appear that Mulgrave's force went into action while he was there. He made a survey of the fortifications and was back in England on 25 July, when he presented his report to the king at Windsor. When Mulgrave returned from Tangier the agitation for the exclusion of his patron, the duke of York, from the succession to the throne was at its height. He opposed the Exclusion Bill in the House of Lords, and was praised by Dryden in *Absalom and Achitophel* under the name of 'sharp-judging *Adriel*' for his firm and manly behaviour as one who was

True to his Prince; but not a Slave of State.

This line may contain a faint hint that, loyal as Mulgrave was,

he had incurred some displeasure at court because of his independent attitude. He appears at this time to have started to
court the Princess Anne, daughter of the king's brother.
A couple of centuries earlier a match between a great noble
and the king's niece would have been regarded as quite
natural, but in the latter part of the seventeenth century the
royal families of Europe were already committed to the
disastrous policy of inbreeding, and poor Anne had to be
wedded to a stupid prince of Denmark. For his presumption
in lifting up his eyes to a princess of the royal blood Mulgrave incurred the king's displeasure, and was deprived of all
his offices in November 1682. However, two years later he
was taken into favour again and was reappointed colonel of
the Old Holland Regiment.

When James II succeeded his brother, Mulgrave, as a
steady Tory and supporter of the king when he was duke of
York, was rewarded by being appointed a member of the
Privy Council on 24 July 1685, and Lord Chamberlain on
20 October. He went to considerable lengths to retain the
favour of the new king. When most of the lords lieutenant
refused to comply with James's unconstitutional proposals,[2]
Mulgrave was one of the few English noblemen who actively
supported the king's policy, and he was rewarded by being
appointed lord lieutenant of the East Riding of Yorkshire in
place of the duke of Somerset in 1687. He also consented to
sit on James's Court of High Commission, though afterwards
he declared that he did not know that this court was illegal.
His *Character of a Tory* is a weak piece of political propa-
ganda in support of James's policy, written as a reply to
Halifax's *Character of a Trimmer*. Mulgrave attended the
king at Mass and knelt with him, but, when the priests tried
to convert him, he showed no disposition to change his
religion. In March 1686, he married Ursula, daughter of a
Somersetshire gentleman and widow of the earl of Conway

and heiress to a great fortune. In 1687 he was corresponding with Etherege, then British envoy at Ratisbon, and the letters that passed between the Lord Chamberlain and the envoy show that they were on excellent terms, in spite of the quarrel between Mulgrave and the Wits which produced *The Essay on Satyr*.

At the Revolution Mulgrave appears to have behaved in a dignified and honourable way. He did his best to help his master, but when it became clear that nothing could save James from the results of his own stupidity he acquiesced in the new order of things and voted for the motion to give the sovereignty jointly to William and Mary. He also deserves credit for the good sense and humanity which he showed in rescuing the Spanish ambassador from the 'No Popery' mob which was wrecking 'mass-houses' and the embassies of Catholic countries on the departure of James.

In the early years of the reign of William III Mulgrave was leader of the Tory opposition in the House of Lords. In January 1692/3, he made an eloquent speech in support of the claim of the Lords to assess their own estates, and in the same year he opposed the Triennial Bill and the attempt to reimpose the censorship of the Press. He passed over to the side of the Government in 1694, when he was made a Privy Councillor by William with a pension of three thousand pounds, and was created Marquess of Normanby. He was admitted to the Cabinet Council in June, and in November was acting as Speaker to the House of Lords during the illness of Lord Somers. Two years later, however, he quarrelled with the Government over the form of words to be used in a pledge designed to support William and Mary against Jacobite attacks. The words to which he objected were a description of William as 'rightful and lawful king', and in consequence he was dismissed from his offices, and went into opposition again during the last years of William's

reign, when he strenuously opposed the attainder of the
Jacobite Sir John Fenwick and the Act of Settlement.

When Anne came to the throne, she at once took her old
admirer into high favour. He was readmitted to the Privy
Council and created Duke of Buckinghamshire and Normanby in March 1702/3. His first wife died in 1697, and in
1699 he married Katherine, the daughter of Fulke Greville,
Lord Brooke, and the widow of the earl of Gainsborough.
This lady died childless early in 1704 and very soon afterwards the Duke married Catherine, Lady Anglesey, the
natural daughter of James II and Katherine Sedley, countess
of Dorchester.[1] Catherine inherited none of the wit of her
mother or of her maternal grandfather. She was only twenty-
five when she married Sheffield, who was then forty-six, and
she had already been married to the earl of Anglesey, whom
she divorced for cruelty. The new Duchess was noted for her
fanatical pride and self-worship. She was nicknamed
'Princess Buckingham' and was the original of Pope's *Atossa*
in *The Characters of Women*.

From an entry in Pepys's Diary we learn that in 1668 Mulgrave had a town house at Charing Cross. Early in the
eighteenth century he bought for thirteen thousand pounds
the lease of the grounds called the Mulberry Garden at the
west end of St James's Park. This garden was originally laid
out by James I for the encouragement of the English silk
trade. In the reign of Charles II it was a public pleasure
ground attached to a tavern and was a favourite resort of the
wits and the women of the town. Adjoining the garden was
a house belonging to Lord Arlington, which was burnt in
1674. On this site Buckinghamshire employed an architect
called Captain Wynne to build him a palatial mansion in
1705. The new Buckingham House became one of the sights
of Queen Anne's London, and the duke describes it in some

[1] See above, p. 37.

detail and with much complacency in his *Letter to the Duke of Shrewsbury* printed in the collected edition of his works published in 1723.

At Buckingham House, 'Princess Buckingham' kept a semi-royal state, and there the duke enjoyed entertaining young men of letters. Among his guests were the young Matthew Prior, poet and diplomatist, and that astonishing youth Alexander Pope, whose brilliant literary craftsmanship was the talk of the town in the early years of Queen Anne's reign. The duke seems to have been kind to Pope, who repaid him with magnificent compliments in verse, though, in conversation with Spence, he described him as 'superficial'. The little, bright-eyed, ironic poet must often have strolled with Buckinghamshire in his spacious gardens, eaten his magnificent dinners; and listened to his stories of the Restoration Court wits.

Sheffield was a politician who always worshipped the rising sun. Just as he looked towards James in the reign of Charles II and towards Anne in the reign of William III, so now he turned his eyes towards Hanover and began corresponding with the Electress Sophia, promising to her and her son Prince George the support of the Tory party. He went further and offended the queen by suggesting that the electress should be invited to come and live in England. When the Whigs gained control of the Government in 1705 they took the Privy Seal away from Buckinghamshire and gave it to the duke of Newcastle, but when the Tories triumphed in 1710 they made him Lord President of the Council as 'one who can never be dangerous'. In 1707 he was one of the commissioners for the Union with Scotland. When the Tories made peace with France he very honourably championed the cause of the Catalans who had risen in rebellion to support the Allies in the war against Louis XIV. He is said to have made strenuous efforts on their behalf and 'got two councils appointed to debate the matter with the queen' after the decision had been taken to sacrifice these unfortunate people who had placed their trust in the honour of the British Government. All his efforts were, however, unavailing and the Catalans were thrown to the wolves.

When Anne died, Buckinghamshire, as Lord President of the Council, was one of the lord justices who ruled England until King George arrived and chose his new ministers. In spite of the duke's previous approaches to the House of Hanover, the new king looked coldly on him, and he was dismissed from all his offices. He lived in retirement for seven years after the accession of George I, dying in 1721, and was buried in Westminster Abbey. An epitaph which he composed for himself was not allowed to be placed on his tomb because it was considered too unorthodox: 'Pro rege sæpe; pro republica semper; improbus vixi; incertus non perturbatus morior. Xtum veneror, in Deo confido æterno ac omnipotente. Ens entium miserere mei.' (Often I served my king, always my country; I lived a sinful life; I die in doubt but not in fear. I revere Christ, I trust in an eternal and omnipotent God. Supreme Being, have pity on me.) This epitaph is by no means the worst of his compositions, and it reflects very well the temper of the agnostic English aristocrat of the eighteenth century.

'Princess' Buckingham, with all her faults, was a loyal wife. She not only erected a sumptuous tomb for her duke but she employed Pope to bring out a magnificent edition of his works in two quarto volumes (published by Alderman Barber) on which no expense was spared to make it one of the handsomest English books of the age. After the death of the duchess, Buckingham House was sold by Sir Charles Sheffield, the duke's natural son, to George III in 1762 for twenty-eight thousand pounds. It stood until 1825, when it was rebuilt as Buckingham Palace by Nashe for George IV.

John Sheffield's character seems to have been a strange compound of arrogance, self-sufficiency, covetousness, fairness, courage and humanity. Macky described him as 'a Nobleman of learning and good natural parts, but of no principles. Violent for the High Church, yet seldom goes to it. Very proud, insolent and covetous and takes all advantages. In paying his debts unwilling, and is neither esteemed nor beloved.' This summary was endorsed by Swift as the truest of all Macky's sketches. On the other hand, the anonymous author of *The Character of John Sheffield Duke of Buckingham* writes that he was 'a good husband, a just and tender father, a constant zealous friend, and one may add the most agreeable of companions'. The truth probably lies between these two descriptions. There must have been something remarkable in a man who could win the praise both of Dryden and of Pope, even if we allow for the natural inclination of men of letters in an aristocratic age to praise a munificent patron.

As a writer Sheffield was absurdly overpraised by his contemporaries. In the latter part of the eighteenth century there was a very natural reaction against this adulation. Horace Walpole, in his *Royal and Noble Authors*, after quoting from *The General Dictionary* the judgment that Sheffield was 'one of the most beautiful prose writers and greatest poets of his age', counters it with his own opinion that 'his grace's compositions in prose have nothing extraordinary in them; his verse is most indifferent, and the greatest part of them is now fallen into neglect'. Dr Johnson's verdict is much fairer and more discriminating: 'Favour and flattery are now at end; criticism is no more softened by his bounties; or awed by his splendour; and, being able to take a steady view, discovers in him a writer that sometimes glimmers, but rarely shines. His songs are upon common topics; he hopes, and grieves, and repents, and despairs, and rejoices, like any other maker of little stanzas; to be great he hardly tries; to be gay is hardly in his power....His verses are often insipid; but his memoirs are lively and agreeable; he had the perspicuity and elegance of a historian, but not the fire and fancy of a poet.' The only part of this judgment with which a modern critic can quarrel is the rather severe condemnation of the songs, which is certainly due to Johnson's dislike of elegant and courtly lyric poetry and particularly of the tradition of the rococo pastoral. Sheffield's poetry has none of the wit and power of Rochester's nor the gaiety of Dorset's or Etherege's, but he has a genuine though slight lyrical gift comparable with, but inferior to, that of Sedley; and, though, as Johnson said, he usually only 'glimmers' rather fitfully, he really does shine in a few songs, such as 'To a Coquet Beauty', 'The Relapse' and the sprightly and melodious 'Dialogue between an Elderly Shepherd and a Very Young Nymph'. Of his poems in the couplet the poorest is *The Essay on Satyr*, which, although it was possibly revised both by Dryden for the edition of 1680 and by Pope for that of 1723, remains a feeble string of invectives with hardly a glimmer of real wit, except in the passage describing the two royal mistresses. The most interesting of the couplet poems are *The Essay on Poetry* and the lines 'To a Lady retiring into a Monastery'. *The Essay on Poetry* is said to have been his own favourite, and he was constantly revising it. It has an historical interest as one of the earliest English attempts at the critical essay in verse and as an expression of critical opinions current in the last decades of the seventeenth century. It was certainly one of the poems which influenced Pope in the composition of his *Essay on Criticism*, where Buckinghamshire is praised as

> The Muse, whose Rules and Practice tell,
> *Nature's chief masterpiece is writing well.*

Buckinghamshire's poems in the couplet represent a transition from the fitful brilliance and gentlemanly negligence of the Restoration Wits to the finished craftsmanship and exquisite polish of Pope. Of his recasting of Shakespeare's *Julius Cæsar* as two neo-classical tragedies with choruses, some of which were written by the young Pope, little need be said. They are 'period pieces', reflecting the taste of the times, like eighteenth-century Shakespeare monuments and busts. The prose of his lively memoirs, essays and letters, however, fully deserves Johnson's praise.

The following passage from his *Letter to the Duke of Shrewsbury*, describing a day in the life of an Augustan grandee, provides a characteristic example of the ease, clarity and distinction of his style:

'To begin then without more preamble: I rise, now in Summer about seven a-clock, from a very large bedchamber (intirely quiet, high, and free from the early sun) to walk in the garden; or, if rainy, in a *Salon* filled with pictures, some good, but none disagreeable; there also, in a row above them, I have many portraits of famous persons in several kinds, as are enough to excite ambition in any man less lazy, or less at ease, than my self.

'Instead of a little dozing closet (according the unwholesome custome of most people) I chuse this spacious room, for all my small affairs, reading books or writing letters; where I am never in the least tired, by the help of stretching my legs sometimes in so long a room, and of looking into the pleasantest park in the world just underneath it.

'Visits, after a certain hour, are not to be avoided; some of which I own a little fatiguing (tho' thanks to the town's lazines, they come pretty late) if the garden was not so near, as to give reasonable refreshment between those ceremonious interruptions. And I am more sorry than my coachman himself, if I am forced to go abroad any part of the morning. For though my garden is such, as by not pretending to rarities or curiosities, has nothing in it to inveagle one's thoughts, yet by advantage of situation and prospect, it is able to suggest the noblest that can be; in presenting at once to view a vast Town, a Palace, and a magnificent Cathedral. I confess the last with all its splendour, has less share in exciting my devotion, than the most common shrub in my garden: For though I am apt to be sincerely devout in any sort of religious assemblies, from the very best (that of our own Church) even to those of *Jews*, *Turks*, and *Indians*: Yet the works of nature appear to me the better sort of sermons; and every flower contains in it the most edifying rhetorick, to fill us with admiration of its omnipotent Creator.

'After I have dined (either agreeably with friends, or at worst with better company than your country-neighbours) I drive away to a Place[1] of air and exercise; which some constitutions are in absolute need of: agitation of the body and diversion of the mind, being a composition for health above all the skill of *Hippocrates*.

'The small distance of this place from *London*, is just enough for recovering my weariness, and recruiting my spirits, so as to make me fitter than before I set out, for either business or pleasure. At the mentioning of the last of these, methinks I see you smile; but I confess my self so changed (which you maliciously, I know, will call decayed) as to my former enchanting delights, that the company I commonly find at home is agreeable enough to make me conclude the evening on a delightful Terrace, or in a Place free from late visits, except of familiar acquaintance.'

Except where another source is indicated, the text of the poems in the following selection is that of Barber's edition of 1723.

[1] 'Marybone' (Buckingham's footnote).

Poems by John Sheffield
Duke of Buckinghamshire

SONG: THE BALLER'S LIFE

They have too many hours that employ 'em
   About Business, Ambition, or News,
While we that know how to enjoy 'em,
   Wish in vain for the time which such blockheads misuse:
They that toyl in impertinent care,
   May strive to be often at leasure;
They cannot be worse than they are;
   But we whose business is pleasure,
Have never a moment to spare.

   With dangerous Damsels we dally,
Till we come to a closer dispute;
   And when we no more Forces can rally,
Our kind foes gives us leave to retire and recruit;
   Then drooping to *Bacchus* we fly,
Who nobly regarding our merits,
   With Succours alwayes is nigh;
And thus reviving our Spirits,
   We love, and we drink till we dye.

From *A Collection of Poems written upon
Several Occasions by Several Persons*, 1672

The Ballers were a set of fast young people mentioned by Pepys in his Diary
on 30 May 1668, where he notes that he heard of their 'dancing naked' with
'my Lady Bennet and her ladies' and 'all the most roguish things in the
world'. ('My Lady Bennet' was the well-known procuress to whom
Wycherley addressed the ironical dedication of *The Plain Dealer*.)

SONG

When cold despair
Would quench my passion, and end all my care,
Then gentle words and gentle sighs recall
   My vanishing hopes which fain would stay;
But stranger fears soon drive my hopes away;
   And back again to grief I fall:
Her favour thus, like Cordials given in vain
To dying men, do but prolong my pain:
   Ah *Gloriana*, why
Like all your other Lovers, may not I
Have leave, alas, soon to despair and dye?
Be rather cruel, than but kind in part,
Hide those soft looks, or shew as soft a Heart.

From A Collection of Poems written upon
Several Occasions by Several Persons (1672)

TO A COQUET BEAUTY

From Wars and Plagues come no such harms,
As from a Nymph so full of Charms,
So much sweetness in her Face,
In her Motions such a Grace,
In her kind inviting Eyes
Such a soft Enchantment lies,
That we please our selves too soon,
And are with vain hopes undone.
After all her softness, we
Are but Slaves, while she is free;
Free, alas, from all desire,
Except to set the World on Fire.

Thou, fair Dissembler, dost but thus
Deceive thy self as well as us;
Like Ambitious Monarchs, thou
Would'st rather force Mankind to bow,
And venture o'er the World to roam,
Than govern with content at home.
But trust me, *Celia*, trust me when
Apollo's self inspires my Pen,
One hour of Love's Delights out-weighs
Whole Years of Universal Praise,
And one Adorer kindly used,
Is of more use, than Crowds refused.

For what does Youth and Beauty serve?
Why more than all your Sex deserve?
Why such soft alluring Arts
To charm our Eyes, and melt our Hearts?
By your loss, you nothing gain;
Unless you love, you please in vain.

From *A Collection of Poems by Several Hands. Most of them
Written by Persons of Eminent Quality*, 1693

THE DREAM

Ready to throw me at the Feet
   Of that fair Nymph whom I adore,
Impatient those Delights to meet,
   Which I enjoy'd the Night before;

By her wonted scornful Brow,
   Soon the fond Mistake I find;
Ixion mourn'd his Error so,
   When *Juno's* form the Cloud resign'd.

Sleep, to make its Charms more priz'd
   Than waking Joys which most prevail,
Had cunningly itself disguis'd
   In a Shape that could not fail.

There my *Celia's* snowy Arms,
   Breasts, and other Parts more dear,
Exposing new and unknown Charms,
   To my transported Soul appear.

Then you so much Kindness show,
   My Despair deluded flies;
And indulgent Dreams bestow
   What your Cruelty denies.

Blush not that your Image, Love
   Naked to my Fancy brought;
'Tis hard, methinks, to disapprove
   The Joys I feel without your Fault.

Wonder not a fancy'd Bliss
   Can such Griefs as mine remove;
That Honour as fantastick is,
   Which makes you slight such constant Love.

The Virtue which you value so,
   Is but a Fancy frail and vain;
Nothing is solid here below,
   Except my Love, and your Disdain.

SONG

From all Uneasie Passions Free,
Revenge, Ambition, Jealousie,
Contented I had been too blest,
If Love and You would let me Rest.
Yet that Dull Life I now Despise;
  Safe from your Eyes,
I fear'd no Griefs, but, Oh, I found no Joys.

Amidst a thousand soft Desires,
Which Beauty moves, and Love inspires;
I feel such pangs of Jealous Fear,
No heart so kind as mine can bear.
Yet I'll defie the worst of harms;
  Such are those Charms,
'Tis worth a Life, to Die within your Arms.

From *A Collection of Poems by Several Hands. Most of them Written by Persons of Eminent Quality*, 1693

THE RELAPSE

Like Children in a starry Night,
    When I beheld those Eyes before,
I gazed with Wonder and Delight,
    Insensible of all their Pow'r.

I play'd about the Flame so long,
    At last I felt the scorching Fire;
My Hopes were weak, my Passion strong,
    And I lay dying with Desire;

By all the Helps of humane Art,
    I just recover'd so much Sense,
As to avoid with heavy Heart,
    The fair, but fatal Influence.

But, since you shine away Despair,
    And now my Sighs no longer shun,
No *Persian* in his zealous Prayer
    So much adores the rising Sun.

If once again my Vows displease,
    There never was so lost a Lover;
In Love, that languishing Disease,
    A sad Relapse we ne'er recover.

THE RECOVERY

Sighing and languishing I lay,
   A Stranger grown to all Delight,
Passing with tedious Thoughts the Day,
   And with unquiet Dreams the Night.

For your dear sake, my only care
   Was how my fatal Love to hide;
For ever drooping with Despair,
   Neglecting all the World beside:

Till, like some Angel from above,
   Cornelia came to my Relief;
And then I found the Joys of Love
   Can make amends for all the Grief.

Those pleasing Hopes I now pursue,
   Might fail, if you could prove unjust;
But Promises for Heav'n and you
   Who is so impious to mistrust?

Here all my Doubts and Troubles end;
   One tender Word my Soul assures;
Nor am I vain, since I depend
   Not on my own Desert, but yours.

A DIALOGUE
SUNG ON THE STAGE
BETWEEN AN ELDERLY SHEPHERD, AND A
VERY YOUNG NYMPH

Shepherd Bright and Blooming as the Spring,
   Universal Love inspiring!
   All our Swains thy Praises sing,
   Ever gazing and admiring.

Nymph Praises in so high a Strain,
   And by such a Shepherd sung,
   Are enough to make me vain,
   Yet so harmless and so young.

Shepherd I should have despair'd among
   Rivals that appear so gayly:
   But your Eyes have made me young
   By their smiling on me daily.

Nymph Idle Boys admire us blindly,
   Are inconstant, wild, and bold;
   And your using me so kindly,
   Is a Proof you are not old.

Shepherd With thy pleasing Voice and Fashion,
   With thy Humour and thy Youth,
   Chear my Soul, and crown my Passion
   Oh, reward my Love and Truth.

Nymph With thy careful Arts to cover
   That which Fools will count a Fault,
   Truest Friend as well as Lover,
   Oh deserve so kind a Thought.

Each a Part first, and then both together

Happy we shall lie possessing,
   Folded in each other's Arms,
Love and Nature's chiefest Blessing
   In the still increasing Charms.

So the dearest Joys of Loving,
   Which scarce Heaven can go beyond,
We'll be ev'ry Day improving,

Shepherd   You more fair, and I more fond.

Nymph   I more fair, and you more fond.

THE ROYAL MISTRESSES

Nor shall the Royal Mistresses* be nam'd;
Too ugly, or too easie to be blam'd;
With whom each rhyming Fool keeps such a pother,
They are as common that way as the other:
While Santering* C[*harles*] betwixt his beastly Brace,
Meets with dissembling still in either place,
Affected Humour, or a painted Face.
In Loyal Libels we have often told him,
How one has Gilted him, the other Sold him.
How that affects to laugh, how this to weep;
But who so long can Rail, as he can Sleep?
Was ever Prince by two at once mis-led,
False, foolish, old, ill-natur'd, and ill-bred?

From *An Essay upon Satyr in The Fourth (and last) Collection
of Poems, Satyrs, Songs, &c.* London, 1689

The history of the famous squib from which this extract is taken is told by
G. R. Noyes and H. R. Mead in their pamphlet *An Essay upon Satyr* . . .
London . . . *Dring* . . . 1680 (University of California Press, 1948). It was circulating in manuscript in November 1679, when it is mentioned in a letter of
Rochester's to Henry Savile. It was first printed in *The Fourth (and Last)
Collection of Poems*, etc. (1689), from which the text of the above extract is
taken. In this collection it is attributed to 'J. D—en Esq.' There is, however,
no doubt that Sheffield was the author of it, and it is included (with many
corrections and alterations by Pope) in the editions of the Duke's works
published in 1723 and 1726. According to a note in these editions it was
written in 1675.

1 *Royal Mistresses:* Barbara Palmer, Duchess of Cleveland, and Louise de
Keroualle, Duchess of Portsmouth.

5 *Santering:* Sheffield in his *Character of Charles II* mentions the king's
addiction to 'a bewitching kind of pleasure called sauntring, and talking
without any constraint . . . the true *Sultana Queen* he delighted in'.

FROM AN 'ESSAY UPON POETRY'

Of Things in which Mankind does most excell,
Nature's chief Master-piece is writing well;
And of all sorts of Writing none there are
Which can the least with *Poetry* compare;
No kind of work requires so nice a touch,
And if well done, there's nothing shine's so much;
But Heav'n forbid we should be so prophane,
To grace the vulgar with that sacred name;
'Tis not a Flash of Fancy which sometimes
Dasling our Minds, sets off the slightest Rimes,
Bright as a blaze, but in a moment done;
True Wit is everlasting, like the Sun;
Which, though sometimes beneath a cloud retir'd,
Breaks out again, and is by all admir'd.
Number, and Rime, and that harmonious sound,
Which never does the Ear with harshness wound,
Are necessary, yet but vulgar Arts,
For all in vain these superficial parts
Contribute to the structure of the whole
Without a Genius too, for that's the Soul;
A Spirit which inspires the work throughout,
As that of Nature moves this World about;
A heat that glows in every word that's writ,
That's something of Divine, and more than Wit;
It self unseen, yet all things by it shown,
Describing all men, but describ'd by none.

From *An Essay upon Poetry*, London, 1682

ON MR HOBBS AND HIS WRITINGS

Such is the Mode of these Censorious Days,
The Art is lost of knowing how to praise;
Poets are envious now, and Fools alone
Admire at Wit, because themselves have none.
Yet, whatsoe'er is by vain Criticks thought,
Praising is harder much than finding fault;
In homely Pieces ev'n the *Dutch* excell,
Italians only can draw Beauty well.

As Strings, alike wound up, so equal prove
That one resounding makes the other move;
From such a cause our Satyrs please so much,
We sympathize with each ill-natur'd touch;
And as the sharp Infection spreads about,
The Reader's Malice helps the Writer out.
To blame, is easy; to commend, is bold;
Yet, if the Muse inspires it, who can hold?
To Merit we are bound to give Applause,
Content to suffer in so just a Cause.

While in dark Ignorance we lay afraid
Of Fancies, Ghosts, and every empty Shade;
Great *Hobs* appear'd, and by plain Reason's Light
Put such fantastick Forms to shamefull Flight.
Fond is their Fear, who think Men needs must be
To Vice enslav'd, if from vain Terrors free;
The Wise and Good, Morality will guide;
And Superstition all the World beside.

In other Authors, tho' the Thought be good
'Tis not sometimes so eas'ly understood;
That Jewel oft unpolish'd has remain'd,
Some Words should be left out, and some explain'd;
So that in search of Sense we either stray,
Or else grow weary in so rough a way.

But here sweet Eloquence does always smile,
In such a choice, yet unaffected Style,
As must both Knowledge and Delight impart,
The Force of Reason, with the Flowers of Art;
Clear as a beautiful transparent Skin,
Which never hides the Blood, yet holds it in:
Like a delicious Stream it ever ran,
As smooth as Woman, but as strong as Man.

    Bacon himself, whose universal Wit
Does Admiration through the World beget,
Scarce more his Age's Ornament is thought,
Or greater Credit to his Country brought.

    While Fame is young, too weak to fly away,
Malice pursues her, like some Bird of Prey;
But once on wing, then all the Quarrels cease;
Envy her self is glad to be at peace,
Gives over, wearied with so high a Flight,
Above her reach, and scarce within her Sight.
Hobbs to this happy pitch arriv'd at last,
Might have look'd down with Pride on Dangers past,
But such the Frailty is of human kind,
Men toil for Fame, which no man lives to find;
Long ripening under-ground this *China* lies;
Fame bears no Fruit, till the vain Planter dies.

    Thus Nature, tir'd with his unusual length
Of Life which put her to her utmost Strength,
Such Stock of wit unable to supply,
To spare her self, was glad to let him die.

Thomas Hobbes died on 2 December 1679 at the age of ninety-one. Aubrey states in his 'Life of Hobbes' (Aubrey's *Brief Lives*, ed. Clark, vol. I, p. 358) that he asked Waller to write some verses in praise of the philosopher, but that he refused because 'he was afrayd of the churchmen'. A broadside *Elegie on Mr Thomas Hobbes lately Deceased* appeared in 1679 (Luttrell Collection B.M. I, 68) but this is not Sheffield's poem, which apparently first appeared in the 1723 edition of his *Works*.

TO A LADY RETIRING INTO A MONASTERY

What Breast but yours can hold the double Fire
Of Fierce Devotion, and of fond Desire?
Love would shine forth, were not your Zeal so bright
Whose glaring Flames eclipse his gentler Light:
Less seems the Faith that Mountains can remove,
Than this, which triumphs over Youth and Love.

But shall some threat'ning Priest divide us two?
What worse than that could all his Curses do?
Thus with a Fright have some resign'd their Breath,
And poorly dy'd only for fear of Death.

Heav'n sees our Passions with Indulgence still,
And they who love well, can do nothing ill.
While to us nothing but ourselves is dear,
Should the World frown, yet what have we to fear?
Fate, Wealth, and Pow'r, those high-priz'd Gifts of Fate,
The low Concerns of a less happy State,
Are far beneath us: Fortune's self may take
Her aim at us, yet no Impression make;
Let Worldlings ask her Help, or fear her Harms;
We can lie safe, lock'd in each other's Arms,
Like the blest Saints, eternal Raptures know,
And slight those Storms that vainly rest below.

Yet this, all this you are resolv'd to quit;
I see my Ruin, and I must submit:
But think, O think, before you prove unkind,
How lost a Wretch you leave forlorn behind.

Malignant Envy, mix'd with Hate and Fear,

There is apparently a connection between this poem and Pope's *Elegy to the Memory of an Unfortunate Lady*. Warburton in his edition of Pope's *Works* published in 1751 appends the following note to the *Elegy* with the initial 'P' to signify that he had it from Pope himself: 'See the Duke of Buckingham's verses to a Lady designing to retire into a Monastery compared with Mr Pope's *Letters to several Ladies*, p. 206. She seems to be the same person whose unfortunate death is the subject of this poem.'

Revenge for Wrongs too burdensome to bear,
Ev'n Zeal itself, from whence all Mischiefs spring,
Have never done so barbarous a Thing.

    With such a Fate the heav'ns decreed to vex
Armida once, tho' of the fairer Sex;
Rinaldo she hath charm'd with so much Art,
Hers was his Pow'r, his Person and his Heart;
Honour's high Thoughts no more his Mind could move,
She sooth'd his Rage, and turn'd it all to Love:
When streight a Gust of fierce Devotion blows,
And in a moment all her Joys o'erthrows:
The poor Armida tears her golden Hair,
Matchless till now for Love, or for Despair.
Who is not mov'd while the sad Nymph complains?
Yet you now act what *Tasso* only feigns;
And after all our Vows, our Sighs, our Tears,
My banish'd Sorrows, and your conquer'd Fears;
So many Doubts, so many Dangers past,
Visions of Zeal must vanquish me at last.

    Thus, in great Homer's War, throughout the Field
Some Hero still made all things mortal yield;
But when a God once took the vanquish'd Side,
The Weak prevail'd, and the Victorious dy'd.

Epilogue

ERTAIN KINDS OF ART only flourish during limited periods. Then they decay and are succeeded by others. For some reason the environment changes and becomes uncongenial. The environment out of which the poetry of the Restoration courtiers grew underwent a change of this kind in the period immediately following the Revolution of 1688. Younger men like George Granville and William Walsh, who tried to reproduce the lives of the Restoration wits and to write in their manner appear to posterity as Young Pretenders, mere pale and ineffectual imitations. By the end of the century the character of the court wit had become the absurdity which Swift exhibits with sardonic gusto in *A Tale of a Tub* when he describes the activities of the three brothers in high society: 'They writ and rallied, and rhymed, and sung and said nothing: they drank, and fought, and whored, and slept, and swore and took snuff: they went to new plays on the first night, haunted the chocolate-houses, beat the watch, lay on bulks, and got claps: they bilked hackney-coachmen, ran into debt with shopkeepers and lay with their wives, kicked fidlers down stairs, eat at *Lockets*, loitered at *Will's*....' The men who did these things in Swift's time were mere micro-coats, imitators of the externals of what had once been a life of gaiety, adventure and poetry. Henry Felton, in his *Dissertation on the Reading the Classics and Forming a Just Style*, written in 1709 for his pupil the young Lord Roos, looks back with admiration at the courtiers for whom literature was not a mere pastime but an indispensable part of a gentleman's equipment: 'After the Court of Augustus, we may mention the Court of King *Charles* II, and find my Lord *Rochester* and *Dorset*, the Duke of *Buckingham* that was then, and the Duke of *Buckingham* that is now, Paramount in Wit, and as Graceful in their Writings, as in their Persons: the Wit of some of them scandalously abused, but otherwise their Satyr was Courtly and their Poetry upon all subjects in the last Perfection....Sir *Robert Howard*, Sir *Charles Sidley*, Sir *John Denham*, Mr *Waller*, Sir *George Etherege*, and I may add Mr *Walsh*, writ like themselves; their Learning and Quality adorn each other, and You may read their Education as Gentlemen, as well as Scholars in their Compositions.'

For two and a half centuries the Puritans and the bacchanalians have done their worst with the reputations of these men. Now the time has come to see them neither as cynical debauchees nor as dashing rakes, but as representatives of the last English courtly civilisation which included a genuine and creative culture.

Bibliography

(This is not a complete bibliography, but a list of short titles
of the principal books used in the preparation of
Restoration Carnival)

GENERAL WORKS

AUBREY, JOHN. *Brief Lives, chiefly of Contemporaries, edited
from the Author's MSS. by Andrew Clark.* Oxford, 1898.

BRYANT, ARTHUR. *King Charles II.* London, 1931.

—— *England in the Reign of Charles II.* London, 1934.

BURNET, GILBERT. *Bishop Burnet's History of His Own Time with
Notes by the Earls of Dartmouth and Hardwick.* Oxford,
1833.

THE DICTIONARY OF NATIONAL BIOGRAPHY.

DOBRÉE, BONAMY. *Restoration Comedy, 1660–1720.* Oxford,
1924.

—— *Rochester a Conversation.* London, 1926.

DRYDEN, JOHN. *The Works of John Dryden, in eighteen volumes,
with notes and a Life of the Author by Walter Scott.* 1808.

—— *The Poetical Works, edited by G. R. Noyes.* Houghton
Mifflin Company, Cambridge, Mass., 2nd (revised) edition,
1950.

EVELYN, JOHN. *The Diary, with an Introduction and Notes by
Austin Dobson, in three volumes.* London, 1906.

FELTON, HENRY. *A Dissertation on Reading the Classics and
Forming a Just Style, written in the year* 1709. *London,
Printed for Jonah Bowyer,* 1715.

HAMILTON, ANTHONY. *Memoirs of Count Grammont, edited by
Gordon Goodwin.* London, 1903.

JOHNSON, SAMUEL. *The Lives of the Poets, edited by G. Birkbeck
Hill.* Oxford, 1920.

KEMP, HOBART. *A Collection of Poems Written upon several
Occasions, by Several Persons.* London, 1672.

LEAVIS, F. R. *Revaluation.* London, 1936.

LOCKER-LAMPSON, FREDERICK. *Lyra Elegantiarum, a collection of
Some of the Best Social and Occasional Verse by Deceased
English Authors, revised and enlarged edition.* London, 1891.

MACAULAY, LORD. *The History of England from the accession of James the Second, edited by Charles Harding Firth.* London, 1913.

MACKY, JOHN. *Memoirs of the Secret Services of John Macky during the reigns of King William, Queen Anne and King George I, by John Macky.* London, 1733.

PALMER, JOHN. *The Comedy of Manners.* London, 1913.

PELTZ, CATHARINE WALSH. 'The Neo-Classic Lyric, 1660–1725.' *Journal of English Literary History*, no. 2, vol. II. Baltimore, June, 1944.

PEPYS, SAMUEL. *The Diary*, edited by Henry B. Wheatley. London, 1928.

POEMS, SATYRS, SONGS: *The Fourth (and Last) Collection of Poems, Satyrs, Songs, etc. Most of which never before printed.* London, 1689.

SAUNDERS, FRANCES. *A Collection of Poems by Several Hands. Most of them Written by Persons of Eminent Quality.* London, 1693.

SPENCE, JOSEPH. *Anecdotes, Observations, and Characters of Books and Men with notes, by S. W. Singer, second edition.* London, 1858.

WALPOLE, HORACE. *A Catalogue of the Royal and Noble Authors of England with Lists of their Works; the Second Edition, corrected and enlarged. London, MDCCXLIX.*

WILSON, JOHN HAROLD. *The Court Wits of the Restoration.* Princeton University Press, Princeton, 1948.

—— *Nell Gwyn Royal Mistress.* Pellegrini and Cudahy, New York, 1952.

WOOD, ANTHONY à. *Athenæ Oxonienses, edited by Phillip Bliss.* London, 1813–1820.

—— *The Life and Times, collected from his Diaries and other Papers by Andrew Clark.* Oxford, 1891.

SIR CHARLES SEDLEY

The Mulberry-Garden A Comedy As it is Acted by His Majestie's Servants, Written by the Honourable Sir Charles Sidley. London. Printed for H. Herringhman, 1668.

Bellamira, or the Mistress, A Comedy: As it is Acted by Their

Majesties Servants. Written by the Honourable Sir Charles Sedley. London: Printed by D. Mallet, for L. C. and Timothy Goodwin, 1687.

The Miscellaneous Works of the Honourable Sir Charles Sedley, Bart. Published from the Original Manuscripts by Capt. Ayloffe. London, 1702.

The Poetical and Dramatic Works of Sir Charles Sedley Collected and Edited from the Old Editions, by V. de Sola Pinto. Constable and Company Ltd., London, 1928.

Sir Charles Sedley 1639–1701, a Study in the Life and Literature of the Restoration by V. de Sola Pinto. Constable and Company Ltd., London, 1927.

The Diary and Letters of Philip Henry. London, 1882.

SIR GEORGE ETHEREGE

The Comical Revenge; or, Love in a Tub. Acted at His Highness the Duke of York's Theatre. London, Printed for Henry Herringman, 1664. (Etherege's name is not on the title page, but the dedication is signed 'Geo. Etherege').

She wou'd if she cou'd, a Comedy. Acted at His Highness the Duke of York's Theatre. Written by George Etherege Esq; London, Printed for H. Herringman, 1668.

The Man of Mode, Or Sr Fopling Flutter. A Comedy. Acted at the Duke's Theatre. By George Etherege Esq; London, Printed for J. Macock, 1676.

The Works of Sir George Etherege: containing his Plays and Poems. London. Printed for H. H. And Sold by J. Tonson, 1704.

The Dramatic Works of Sir George Etherege Edited with an Introduction and Notes by H. F. B. Brett-Smith. Oxford: Basil Blackwell, 1927.

The Letter Book of Sir George Etherege, Minister at Ratisbon, 1685–1688. Brit. Mus. Add. MS 11513.

The Letterbook of Sir George Etherege Edited with an Introduction and Notes by Sybil Rosenfield. Oxford, 1928.

Notes on Sir George Etherege by Miss D. FOSTER in *Notes and Queries*, 10, 17, 24 and 31 December 1927, and in *Review of English Studies*, VIII, October, 1932.

CHARLES SACKVILLE, EARL OF DORSET

The Works of the most Celebrated Minor Poets. Volume the First. Containing the Works of Wentworth, Earl of Roscommon; Charles, Earl of Dorset; Charles, Earl of Halifax; Sir Samuel Garth. London: Printed for F. Cogan, MDCCXLIX.

A Supplement to the Works of the Minor Poets. Part I (n.d.).

Poems on Affairs of State from Oliver Cromwell. Part III With other Miscellany Poems. 1698.

Charles Sackville Sixth Earl of Dorset Patron and Poet of the Restoration, by Brice Harris. The University of Illinois Press, Urbana, 1940.

JOHN WILMOT, EARL OF ROCHESTER

Poems on Several Occasions. By the Right Honourable, the E. of R—. Printed at Antwerp, 1680. (Facsimile reprint of the Huntington Library copy edited by James Thorpe, Princeton, 1950.)

Poems on Several Occasions. Written by a Late Person of Honour. London Printed for A. Thorncome, 1685.

Valentinian: A Tragedy As 'tis Alter'd by the Late Earl of Rochester. London: Printed for Timothy Goodwin, 1685.

Poems &c. on Several Occasions: With Valentinian, A Tragedy. Written by the Right Honourable John Late Earl of Rochester. London, Printed for Jacob Tonson, 1691.

The Collected Works of John Wilmot Earl of Rochester Edited by John Hayward. The Nonesuch Press, MCMXXVI.

Poems by John Wilmot Earl of Rochester edited with an introduction and notes by Vivian de Sola Pinto. London: Routledge and Kegan Paul, 1953.

The Rochester-Savile Letters 1671–1680. Edited by John Harold Wilson. Columbus, The Ohio State University Press, 1941.

A Sermon Preached At the Funeral of the Rt Honourable John Earl of Rochester, by Robert Parsons M.A. Oxford. 1680.

Some Passages of the Life and Death of the Right Honourable John Earl of Rochester, by Gilbert Burnet, D.D. London, 1680.

John Wilmot Earl of Rochester His Life and Writings, by Johannes Prinz. Leipzig, 1927.

Rochesteriana, Being Some Anecdotes Concerning John Wilmot Earl of Rochester Collected and Edited by Johannes Prinz. Leipzig, 1926.

Rochester, Portrait of a Restoration Poet, by Vivian de Sola Pinto. London: John Lane, The Bodley Head, 1935.

Rochester, by Charles Williams. London: Arthur Barker Ltd., 1935.

Articles by J. H. WILSON in *Review of English Studies*:

 'Rochester, Dryden and the Rose Alley Affair' (*R.E.S.*, xv, 59, July, 1939, together with Note by V. DE S. PINTO in *R.E.S.*, xvi, 62, April, 1940).

 'Rochester's Marriage' (*R.E.S.*, xix, 76, October, 1943).

'Rochester and Dr Bendo', anonymous article in *The Times Literary Supplement*, 20 June, 1942.

JOHN SHEFFIELD, DUKE OF BUCKINGHAMSHIRE

An Essay upon Poetry, 1682.

The Works of John Sheffield Earl of Mulgrave, Marquis of Normanby, and Duke of Buckingham, London: Printed for John Barber, and Sold by the Booksellers of London and Westminster, 1723. (Two volumes edited by Pope. The second volume was to have included *Some Account of the Revolution* and *The Feast of the Gods*, but these two pieces were excised by the Government because of their supposed Jacobite tendency. They were, however, printed separately in 1727.)

The Works of John Sheffield, Earl of Mulgrave, Marquis of Normanby, and Duke of Buckingham: Printed for John Barber, Alderman of London, MDCCXXVI.

Miscellanea from the Works of John Sheffield Duke of Buckingham. The Haworth Press, 1933 (The Courtier's Library).

A Character of John Sheffield, late Duke of Buckinghamshire, with an account of the pedigree of the Sheffield family, 1729.

Index of First Lines

Index of First Lines